NEW YORK CITY
AT NIGHT

A TOUR OF THE CITY THAT NEVER SLEEPS

NEW YORK CITY
AT NIGHT
A TOUR OF THE CITY THAT NEVER SLEEPS

PHOTOGRAPHY BY
Evan Joseph

TEXT BY
Marcia Reiss

THUNDER BAY
P·R·E·S·S

San Diego, California

Thunder Bay Press
An imprint of the Baker & Taylor Publishing Group
10350 Barnes Canyon Road, San Diego, CA 92121
www.thunderbaybooks.com

Produced by Salamander Books,
an imprint of Anova Books Ltd.
10 Southcombe Street, London W14 0RA, UK

All notations of errors or omissions should be addressed to Thunder Bay Press,
Editorial Department, at the above address. All other correspondence (author
inquiries, permissions) concerning the content of this book should be addressed
to Salamander Books, 10 Southcombe Street, London W14 0RA, UK.

All photographs by Evan Joseph Uhlfelder, except
for pages 8–15 (see page 144 for details).

Library of Congress Cataloging-in-Publication Data

Reiss, Marcia
  New York City at night / Marcia Reiss.
    p. cm.
  ISBN-13: 978-1-60710-113-0
  ISBN-10: 1-60710-113-0
  1. New York (N.Y.)--Pictorial works. 2. Historic sites--New York (State)--New York--
Pictorial works. 3. New York (N.Y.)--Buildings, structures, etc.--Pictorial works.
4. Night photography--New York (State)--New York. I. Title.
  F128.37.R35 2010
  974.7'1--dc22

                        2010014709

Color Reproduction by Rival Colour Limited, UK
Printed in China by 1010 Printing International Limited

1 2 3 4 5 14 13 12 11 10

CONTENTS

INTRODUCTION

From gas lamps to electric lightbulbs, neon signs and giant video screens, New York has always been a city of light. Broadway's Great White Way began with gas lamps in 1826, and the lights kept getting brighter as the theater district moved up from the Bowery to Forty-second Street. But the city's nighttime glow radiates far beyond Times Square. Ever since the Times Tower celebrated its opening in 1904 with a searchlight on top of the building, the New York skyline began to take its brilliant shape. And once the top of the Empire State Building became a landmark beacon in the 1960s, every building wanted to stand in its own spotlight.

New York's great architecture is artistically flooded with light. From St. Paul's Chapel, Manhattan's oldest building in continuous use, through classical courthouses and museums and Art Deco and modern masterpieces, the nighttime skyline is the city's history in light. It displays more than just buildings: the great bridges, expansive airports, and huge ballparks, as well as the extraordinary places where the absence of buildings is all the more remarkable—the twinkling lights of Central Park's lush oasis, the shimmering glaze on rivers and harbors, and the strange glow of ground zero.

New York City at Night presents all of these places—and the stories behind them—in a wonderful new light. Far from typical photos, these images show the city from new perspectives, both on the street and from exciting aerial angles. The talented photographer Evan Joseph has captured the magic of New York City's evenings. Walking through the neighborhoods and hovering overhead in a helicopter, he has seized the city's blaze of nighttime light and its surreal blue radiance in the few moments between sunset and black velvet skies. His photographs preserve a dynamic city in the midst of its constant, brilliant change.

Marcia Reiss

NEW YORK CITY: A HISTORY

Below: *The Dutch settlement of New Amsterdam, shown on this mid-seventeenth-century map, covered Manhattan's southern tip, barely the island's big toe. The large quadrangular structure on the far left is Fort Amsterdam. Its construction in 1625 is considered the founding date of New York City. On the far right is Wall Street, the site of an actual wall built as a line of defense against Indian attacks and encroaching English colonists. A canal ran down Broad Street into the East River. The letters mark the sites of breweries and taverns, an ample number for the small colony.*

LIGHTING UP NEW YORK

Recognized around the world, New York City's glittering profile owes its origin to a bold inventor in New Jersey. In September 1878, Thomas Edison told a reporter from the *New York Sun* that he had invented a working electric lightbulb. "I have it now," he boasted. But he didn't have it. Inventors had been trying for fifty years to create incandescent electric bulbs that would burn for more than a few minutes. It would be another four years before Edison was able to make good on his promise. He knew that the secret to lighting up cities lay not only in perfecting a long-lasting lightbulb, but also in developing generators and transmission lines to carry electricity from power plants to homes and businesses. Backed by J. P. Morgan and other New York City financiers, he formed the Edison Electric Illuminating Company in 1878 and began to build the city's first major power station at Pearl Street in Lower Manhattan. On September 4, 1882, Edison switched on the Pearl Street generators, illuminating 400 lightbulbs for eighty-five paying customers in New York. The city's nights would never be the same again.

DUTCH BEGINNINGS

Edison was not only a scientist but also an astute and determined businessman. While he was not a native New Yorker, he claimed to be of Dutch ancestry, and his story is reminiscent of the fearless Dutch settlers who laid the foundation for New York City's aggressive lead in trade and commerce. The Dutch were not the first European explorers to venture into New York Harbor. That voyage was made by Giovanni da Verrazano in 1524. But he got no farther than the entrance to the harbor, near the site of the bridge that now bears his name, before sailing back into the Atlantic.

The Dutch East India Company hired Henry Hudson, an Englishman, to find a passage to Asia, and in 1609 he sailed from the harbor up the North River, later called the Hudson, as far as today's state capital of Albany. Dutch fur traders followed and settled in Lower Manhattan in 1613. Within a few decades, the settlement had spread beyond Manhattan to what would become the four outer boroughs of Brooklyn, Queens, Staten Island, and the Bronx. At its height, New Netherland encompassed all or parts of five future states, including New York, New Jersey, Connecticut, Pennsylvania, and Delaware. In 1653 the settlement known as New Amsterdam was granted autonomy as a separate municipality. From the start, it was a bustling, multiethnic microcosm of the future New York City, an unusually mixed society of different religions and races.

Although New Netherland's director-general, Peter Stuyvesant, tried to ban Jews and Quakers and impose Calvinist restrictions on other religions, his superiors at the Dutch West India Company insisted on an official policy of tolerance. They did so to further what would become another great American tradition—capitalism. New Amsterdam was a city of traders who took advantage of Manhattan's deep, sheltered harbor and access to inland rivers. Its 500 colonists spoke eighteen different languages and just about everyone bought shares in the shipments of goods sent back to the Netherlands, including merchants, tradesmen, and even prostitutes. The Dutch were practical businessmen who accepted this polyglot population as a given for doing business in the New World.

New York's Native Americans, however, did not fare as well. The tale that the Dutch acquired Manhattan from the Lenape Indians in exchange for $24 worth of goods may be just a legend, but even considering inflation over the past 400 years, it would have been a raw deal at any price. At the time of the Dutch settlement, the Lenape population of the region was about 15,000. By 1700 it had dropped to 200.

THE BRITISH TAKE CONTROL

By the 1660s, the British colonies of New England and Virginia were encroaching on New Netherland. The British monarch Charles II had designs on the Dutch colony and dispatched John Winthrop, the governor of the Connecticut colony, to make Stuyvesant an offer he could not refuse. On September 4, 1664, the two men confronted each other at the southern tip of Manhattan, near today's Battery Park. Backed by a British flotilla of four ships and 2,000 men, Winthrop rowed ashore and handed Stuyvesant a letter offering terms for the colony. Belligerent but outnumbered, Stuyvesant had no choice but to surrender. Charles's brother James, the Duke of York (and later King James II), had worked behind the scenes in the takeover. He was granted title over the colony, which was soon renamed in his honor.

The Dutch took back the island in 1673, renaming it New Orange, but by 1674 the British were back in control. New York's English governors worked cooperatively with prominent Dutch families whose wealth and landholdings grew with the relationship. Under the first decades of British rule, the Dutch held on to their culture. The streets of New York, with stepped gable-end houses and tiled roofs, continued to look like the streets of Holland. Despite the English laws in favor of male heirs, Dutch women kept their surnames and their right to inherit property. English ways eventually took root, but not without conflicts between the two cultures that erupted from time to time throughout the seventeenth century.

Anglicans were a minority in 1698 when Trinity Church, New York's first Church of England, was built on Broadway and Wall Street. Determined to Anglicize New York, the English governor gave Trinity a large swath of Manhattan real estate that the church still enjoys today. The majority of New Yorkers at the time were Protestant dissenters not affiliated with the Church of England. But over time, prominent Dutch families—Roosevelts, Van Cortlandts, Beekmans, and others whose names ring with impressive familiarity in today's New York—embraced the Anglican Church.

Only a fraction of Lower Manhattan was built up by the end of the seventeenth century, and Trinity's steeple towered over the tiny, densely packed city. The Dutch had built an actual wall on Wall Street to defend New Amsterdam against Indians and encroaching English colonists. The English demolished it and used the stones for the foundation of the colonial city hall, built in 1700 at Wall and Broad streets. In the eighteenth century, the city

expanded as its prosperity grew with Britain's West Indian sugar trade. Both economies were based on slavery. Slaves who worked the farms on Staten Island, the Bronx, and Brooklyn grew food for slaves on the West Indian sugar plantations. New York ships brought food and supplies to the plantations. Shipbuilding docks and sugar refineries were built on the Lower Manhattan waterfront as New York laid the foundation for its role as a world port.

PRELUDE TO REVOLUTION

Prosperity stimulated an increasing demand for labor, both African slaves and new arrivals from Europe. New York's first big wave of immigration surged in the early eighteenth century as German and Irish refugees from European wars, persecution, and famine poured into the colony. Many

Below: *Famous for his wooden leg and stern demeanor, Peter Stuyvesant, the Dutch director-general of New Amsterdam, is portrayed here furiously refusing to sign the English proposal for taking over the colony in 1664. Although he made a great show of his opposition, shocking his fellow Dutchmen around the table, the overwhelming presence of the British fleet in the harbor gave him little choice but to surrender. He eventually returned to New York, where he spent the rest of his life. He is buried in a vault in St. Mark's Church in the East Village, the former site of his farm.*

Right: *By 1835, New York City was at great risk for fire. Rapid growth had packed buildings closely together as the city expanded northward, relying on a woefully inadequate water supply. On the evening of December 16, high winds quickly spread a local fire throughout the Financial District and frigid temperatures froze the water in firemen's hoses. The fire destroyed 674 commercial buildings, including the New York Stock Exchange, yet caused only two deaths. But the city's economic boom, fueled by the 1825 opening of the Erie Canal, continued. New buildings rose in stone and brick, and in 1842 the Croton Aqueduct was completed, establishing a new, reliable water supply. The fire of 1835 would be the city's last great fire.*

Far right: *From the heart of the city to its very edge, New York was a dramatically different place in the mid-nineteenth century than it is today. Manhattan's tallest building was Trinity Church, whose steeple can be seen rising above Lower Broadway in the center of this map from the 1850s. The round structure off the tip of the island is Castle Clinton. Perched on an artificial island, it would later be surrounded by landfill that extended Manhattan's waterfront into the harbor. In the right foreground is Governors Island, expanded in 1900 with landfill to more than twice the size shown here. The fort on its edge, Castle Williams, was built to deter the British in the War of 1812. On the far right is Brooklyn, an independent city until 1898. Without bridges crossing the surrounding rivers, New Yorkers depended on boats of all kinds to travel to and from Manhattan.*

THE GREAT FIRE OF THE CITY OF NEW-YORK, 16 DECEMBER 1835.

arrived as indentured servants. As Britain's economy rode waves of prosperity and recession, it demanded more revenue from its colonies. The economic pressures led to more taxes, corruption, and calls for liberty. One of the most resounding was made in 1735 in defense of the German-born printer John Peter Zenger. Zenger was on trial for libel after he printed a newspaper attack on the New York governor for election fraud and other abuses of justice. Zenger was acquitted by an eloquent plea that would echo forty years later in the War for Independence. "It is not the cause of a poor printer, nor of New York alone," his lawyer proclaimed. "It is the cause of liberty."

Zenger's imprisonment and trial took place at the colonial city hall, the scene of another critical prelude to revolution and the first case of organized opposition to British law. In 1765 Parliament passed the Stamp Act, requiring revenue stamps to be purchased and affixed to virtually all paper sold in the colonies, from newspapers to legal documents. The act violated the colonists' belief that only representatives of their own choosing could impose taxes. Delegates from nine colonies convened at the city hall and raised the cry of "No taxation without representation." After months of boycotts of British businesses and violent demonstrations by the newly formed

Sons of Liberty, Parliament repealed the notorious act in 1766. But restless colonists did not look back from the path toward revolution, and ten years later the War for Independence began.

A NEW BEGINNING

New York came under British attack at the start of the war and fell soon after. Greatly outnumbered, George Washington's troops suffered tremendous losses in the Battle of Brooklyn and might have lost the war at its outset but for Washington's bold maneuver across the fog-shrouded East River from Brooklyn Heights to Manhattan in August 1776. After a brief stand at Harlem Heights, he escaped with his

remaining forces across the Hudson to New Jersey. It would be seven years before he set foot on Manhattan again—in a triumphal return up Broadway.

After the American victory, New York's colonial city hall was renamed Federal Hall and the city became the first U.S. capital. On March 4, 1789, the newly constituted U.S. Congress held its first meeting at Federal Hall to count the votes that declared Washington the first U.S. president. He was inaugurated in front of the building on April 30, 1789. Afterward, he and the members of Congress walked the few blocks to St. Paul's Chapel on Broadway to offer their prayers for the new republic. Thirteen years earlier, a month after Washington had been forced to retreat from New York,

Above: *Violent riots erupted in Manhattan in July 1863 in opposition to new laws drafting men to fight in the Civil War. The outbreak, which lasted for several days, was the largest civil insurrection in American history apart from the war itself. It was led by working-class men who resented the exemption for those who could afford to pay their way out of conscription. But it soon turned against African Americans, targeted as the cause of the war. Countless numbers were brutally murdered in the streets before federal troops finally quelled the mob.*

a fire had engulfed British-occupied New York, destroying more than 500 homes, a fourth of the city's buildings. Trinity Church was consumed but its outpost, St. Paul's, half a dozen blocks to the north, survived. It is intact today with the presidential seal still on Washington's pew. Miraculously, it would survive once again on September 11, 2001, after the World Trade Center towers collapsed directly across the street from the church.

A CITY OF CAPITAL

New York's role as the nation's capital ended only a year later when Philadelphia took the honor in 1790. But New York soon became a city of capital. It had an active securities market as early as 1790, the year the new U.S. secretary of the treasury, Alexander Hamilton, issued bonds to pay for debts incurred in the Revolution. The city experienced tremendous growth in the 1790s, and by 1811 the common council developed a street grid to allow for expansion throughout Manhattan. In that same year, the government

moved into a newly completed city hall on Broadway and Park Row, near the grounds where rebellious colonists had been hanged on British gallows.

Trade exploded after 1825 when the opening of the Erie Canal connected the New York port to the nation's interior. Barges loaded with grain from Midwestern farms clustered around the tip of Manhattan and on the Brooklyn waterfront. Brooklyn sprouted towering storage elevators filled with grain for shipment to Europe. Renewed prosperity brought new waves of immigrants seeking jobs. Eight million, mostly from northern and western Europe, arrived between 1855 and 1890. The Irish, pushed out of their homeland by the potato famine that began in 1845, already comprised a fourth of New York's population by 1850. Their leaders formed Tammany Hall, a political machine that would dominate city politics throughout the second half of the nineteenth century. Thousands of Irish Catholic New Yorkers contributed pennies to begin the construction of St. Patrick's Cathedral in 1858. Many of them earned their money by building Central Park, another monumental project that began a year later. Thousands of workers hauled earth and stone and built a complex system of carriage roads, bridges, and arches to create a pastoral landscape on the wild outskirts of northern Manhattan. The Civil War (1861–65) delayed but did not derail the completion of these magnificent projects.

The Civil War tested New York's patriotism and exposed its racial and class divisions. Its business interests, including shippers and traders in cotton, tobacco, and rice, had strong ties to the South's slave economy. Although Abraham Lincoln delivered one of the most important speeches of his career at New York's Cooper Union in 1860, he did not carry the city in either of his two elections as president in 1860 and 1864. New York's working classes feared competition from free blacks and deeply resented the draft laws that allowed the wealthy to buy their way out of conscription. The anger exploded in the violent draft riots of 1863 when federal troops had to be called to halt three days of anarchy and brutal attacks on blacks.

Although the draft riots left lasting scars, the city rebounded in the postwar economic boom as it had done after the fire and British occupation during the Revolution. Trinity Church, rebuilt in 1846, had dominated the skyline up to the time of the Civil War. In 1869 the towers of the Brooklyn Bridge began to rise and would remain the tallest structures in Lower Manhattan for years after the bridge opened in 1883. Farther uptown, the twin spires of St. Patrick's, completed in 1888, rose even higher.

The Statue of Liberty raised her torch in 1886, a time when immigration from southern and eastern Europe began to surge. The city's first immigration center was at Castle Clinton in Battery Park, but as the flow of people increased, a new, larger center was built on Ellis Island. Twelve million immigrants would pass through Ellis Island from its opening in 1892 to its closing in 1954.

Spreading in all directions and swelled by a growing population, the New York area was controlled by a complicated network of forty local governments that made it difficult for big businesses to expand. Shipping and railroad interests proposed consolidation under a

Below: *Times Square was ablaze with lights in the 1920s, the heyday of the Broadway Theater District. In 1927–28 alone, the electric marquees of seventy-six theaters twinkled with the names of 264 shows. Vaudeville music halls and burlesque shows added to the glittering display.*

centralized government. Brooklyn, long an independent city, resisted but eventually gave in to the irresistible lure of sharing Manhattan's real-estate taxes. After years of debate, consolidation was narrowly approved by popular vote in 1898. The new five-borough city immediately became the most extensive and populous metropolis in the nation. By this time, half of its population was foreign-born.

A CITY ON THE MOVE

At the start of the twentieth century, New York's transportation networks expanded exponentially. The first subway system opened in 1904, and two grand railroad stations soon followed: Penn Station (1910) was connected to a new tunnel under the Hudson River, and Grand Central Terminal (1913) was the crowning glory of Cornelius Vanderbilt's New York Central Railroad.

The city was also bustling with entertainment under the spreading glow of nighttime lights. The Great White Way had begun in 1826 with the installation of 120 gas lamps on Lower Broadway from the Bowery to Grand Street. Previously lit by oil lamps, this was the start of the Broadway Theater District that would continue its march uptown to Forty-second Street. Broadway from Fourteenth to Thirty-fourth streets got its first electric streetlights under new arc lamps in 1880. Installed by the Brush Electric Company, they would soon be replaced by Edison's incandescent bulbs. The far reaches of Brooklyn also burned brightly when Luna Park (1903) and Dreamland (1904) opened on Coney Island, each outlined by more than a million lightbulbs. A vibrant nightlife was also onstage at Harlem's Apollo Theater. Built in 1914 as a whites-only burlesque emporium, it would become the premier venue for top African American entertainers such as Billie Holiday and Duke Ellington in the 1930s and 1940s.

TOWERING CITY

New York was literally moving upward in the first decade of the twentieth century as skyscrapers created a new skyline and a new identity for the city, raising Manhattan's profile from Wall Street to Midtown. The Flatiron Building, the first tower to soar north of City Hall, launched New York's skyscraper era in 1903. When the New York Times moved up from Lower Manhattan to the Times Tower at Forty-second Street, its celebratory fireworks display on New Year's Eve 1904 signaled the start of a brilliant future for

Left: *The 1939–40 World's Fair in New York included 375 buildings, many of them futuristic, but none as iconic as the Trylon and Perisphere. Thousands of visitors lined up to enter the 610-foot-tall Trylon tower and the 180-foot-diameter Perisphere. The construction of the fair reclaimed a 1,200-acre dump on Flushing Bay in Queens. Called a "valley of ashes," the dump was a climactic setting in F. Scott Fitzgerald's 1925 novel* The Great Gatsby. *Mired in the Great Depression and worried about the war, New Yorkers and tourists welcomed the fair as a vision of a better life.*

Far left: *Coney Island was at its brightest from 1897 to 1904 when three fabulously flashy amusement parks—Steeplechase, Dreamland, and Luna Park—opened on the oceanfront in southern Brooklyn. This is Luna Park, called the "Electric Eden," a storybook city of minarets, domes, and spires outlined with more than a million electric lightbulbs. Filled with fantastic rides, it drew crowds until the mid-twentieth century, when it was replaced by a housing development.*

Times Square. But downtown was not forsaken. The sixty-story Woolworth Building facing City Hall Park became the world's tallest building in 1913. It kept that title until 1930 when the Chrysler Building claimed it—for less than a year. The Empire State Building took the honor in 1931. The same year saw the opening of the George Washington Bridge. More than twice the length of the Brooklyn Bridge, it was the longest suspension bridge of its day. Even during the worst years of the Depression, New York had something to look up to in Rockefeller Center, the largest private real-estate venture ever undertaken in the city.

After World War II, as other world capitals lay damaged or in ruins, New York emerged as the world's leading city. The United Nations Secretariat Building (1947–53) embodied this fact. It established New York as the international capital and also ushered in a new era of modern architecture. The 1964 World's Fair reinforced New York's global prominence with the Unisphere, a twelve-story steel replica of the globe that still stands in Flushing Meadows Park in Queens.

New York looked much worse during its financial near-collapse of the 1970s, and the twenty-five-hour power blackout on July 13, 1977, made this period even darker. But the 1980s brought financial recovery and a new building boom. Two of the city's iconic attractions that had fallen into squalid disrepair, Central Park and Times Square, look better than ever today. Since the loss of the World Trade Center towers in 2001, New York has continued to rebound as it has done since its earliest travails. New buildings are rising at ground zero and resilient New Yorkers have returned to live all around it. In 1697 the streets of New York were so dark that an ordinance was passed requiring home owners to hang out lanterns. Today, even the occupants of the International Space Station 300 miles above the city can see the bright lights of New York.

Left and above: *Ever since she came on the scene in 1886, the Statue of Liberty has been New York's most famous lady, a colossal figure more than 150 feet tall, or twice that if one counts the height of her pedestal. Since she faces New York, views of her face have New Jersey in the background. Stories differ as to the inspiration for her classical features. Credit is given to both the mother of the statue's sculptor, Frederic Bartholdi, and the attractive wife of an American industrialist who lived in France, where the statue was created. Bartholdi's mistress was said to be the model for Liberty's arms. The statue got a total makeover for her centennial on July 4, 1986, including a new torch and steel replacements for much of her iron skeleton, originally crafted by Alexandre Gustave Eiffel, who designed the Eiffel Tower in 1889. Closed after the World Trade Center attacks of 2001, the statue's home on Liberty Island did not reopen until 2004. Today, visitors strong enough to climb up the 354 steps inside the statue can reserve small group tours to see amazing views from inside her crown.*

Right: *Twelve million immigrants entered America through Ellis Island from its opening as a federal immigration center in 1892 to its closing in 1954. But they were not the only immigrants arriving during this period. For the most part, the twelve million came here as steerage or third-class passengers to undergo inspections in the Great Hall, the large building with the corner turrets. First- and second-class passengers, considered less likely to become medical or economic burdens in America, were given a cursory inspection aboard the ships. Immigration declined in the 1920s when strict quotas were established, limiting the number of people from certain countries. Once Ellis Island closed, the buildings deteriorated, even after it was declared a national monument in 1965, because Congress did not appropriate restoration funds. The Ellis Island Foundation, established in 1982, raised millions in corporate and private funds and reopened the Great Hall as a museum in 1990. Today, 100 million Americans, a third of the nation's population, can trace their ancestry to someone who arrived at Ellis Island.*

Left: *Once the Dutch settled here in the seventeenth century, they began to add real estate by extending the shoreline with landfill. When Peter Stuyvesant stood at the tip of Manhattan in 1664 to meet John Winthrop, the British governor arriving by ship to demand the surrender of New Amsterdam, neither of them actually stood at the tip shown here but rather, a few hundred feet back at the shoreline as it then existed. The swath of land that is now Battery Park (left), the Staten Island Ferry Terminal next to it (on the right), and virtually all of the waterfront land circling Manhattan Island are the product of landfill. The process continued into the 1970s when the excavated rock and soil for the World Trade Center foundations were used to create the adjacent Battery Park City, the stretch of land going up the Hudson to the left of Battery Park. Like all Manhattan skyscrapers, the towers at the water's edge are deeply anchored into bedrock below the fill.*

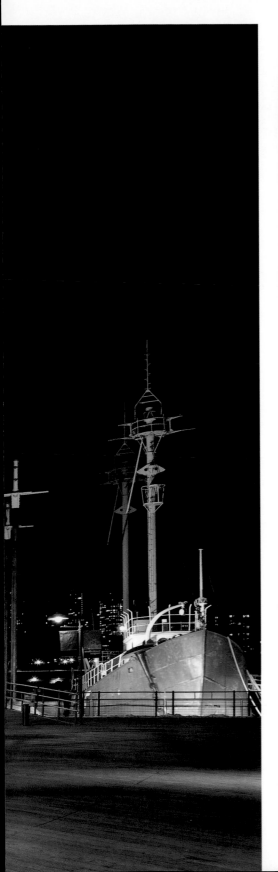

Left: *When ships loaded with cargo docked here at South Street, the neighborhood was a rowdy place of maritime shops, boardinghouses, saloons, and brothels. It has been nearly a century since the ships moved to other parts of the harbor, and the area has clearly changed. In 1967 a citizens' group formed the South Street Seaport Museum, gathered a fleet of historic ships, and convinced the city to landmark the area as the South Street Seaport Historic District, covering three piers and a dozen blocks of nineteenth-century buildings just south of the Brooklyn Bridge. It was the first time in the city's history that urban renewal focused on preserving rather than demolishing historic buildings. Pier 17 (seen here), built in 1985, is a three-story structure filled with shops and restaurants.*

Above: *With one of the world's largest maritime collections, the South Street Seaport Museum has historic ships both large and small. It includes more than 1,000 ship models like this three-masted beauty, seen here in a workshop with a shiplike setting. Visitors can also see working presses in the nineteenth-century print shop and explore the archaeology museum and marine life conservation laboratory. One can climb aboard the full-size ships docked on the nearby piers and enjoy a sail on the East River in good weather.*

Left: *Surrounded by rivers, New York is a city of dramatic contrasts—towering buildings against a backdrop of striking scenery marked by centuries of change. In the foreground is the Hudson River and the Lower Manhattan waterfront lined with the towers of two enormous projects built in the 1980s: Battery Park City and the World Financial Center. Behind them is ground zero, the open space flooded with light. The brightly lit towers on the left are recent developments, signs of*

resurgence in this damaged area: Goldman Sachs's new headquarters (2010) is on the far left, and to its immediate right is Seven World Trade Center (2006). The top of the Woolworth Building (1913) rises above Seven World Trade Center. On the far right is the tallest tower on Wall Street, the former Cities Service Building (1932). In the background is the East River and its famous crossings: the Brooklyn Bridge (1883) and the Manhattan Bridge (1909).

Above: *Across the street from ground zero, the World Financial Center buildings have been operating again for several years and a new tower was completed in 2010. This area includes the offices of the nation's leading financial companies, including Merrill Lynch, Dow Jones, American Express, and the Wall Street Journal. The brightly lit tower is the new global headquarters of Goldman Sachs. The broad highway on the right is West Street, crossed by two*

pedestrian bridges. Damaged in the fall of the twin towers in 2001, the bridges are open once again. Many of the commuters to and from this busy area ferry across the Hudson River (left) between Manhattan and New Jersey.

Left: *Empty space is an urban anomaly, and the continued presence of this gaping hole in the center of Lower Manhattan is a constant reminder of the tragedy of September 11, 2001. Yet this sixteen-acre pit belies years of activity. Below the surface, the vast infrastructure that was destroyed along with the twin towers has been restored. The subway is running again between the World Trade Center Station and New Jersey. New retaining walls and electrical, plumbing, and communication cables have been laid for future construction. The glass-walled, flattop building on the far left is Seven World Trade Center, the first tower in the complex to rise again. Completed in 2006, it replaced a damaged building that fell soon after the twin towers. A memorial park and underground museum are also under construction. Most important, the steel framework for One World Trade Center, the tower that will reach 1,776 feet, symbolic of the year of American Independence, is rising on the site. However, progress still moves at a slow pace: the building is not expected to be completed until 2013.*

Right: *The World Trade Center towers once stood in the now-empty sky behind St. Paul's Chapel. Miraculously, the historic chapel, built in 1764, was not damaged when the towers fell. Its graveyard was covered by debris, but the chapel immediately became a respite center for rescue volunteers and stayed open twenty-four hours a day for the next nine months while the volunteers searched ground zero for victims' remains. Its wooden pews still bear the scuff marks left by the heavy boots of those who slept there between their work shifts. One of the carefully protected pews belonged to President George Washington, who worshipped here in the brief period from 1789 to 1790 when New York City was the nation's capital. The presidential seal still hangs on the wall above the pew.*

Left: *Located directly across the street from ground zero, the beautiful structure of the Winter Garden was severely damaged during the fall of the World Trade Center. Debris from the falling towers crushed part of the steel frame, and the impact of the collapse blew out nearly all of the glass in the barrel-vaulted arch. The building reopened just a year later in September 2002, with 2,000 new panes of glass, 60,000 square feet of new marble flooring and stairs, and sixteen new palm trees, each forty feet tall. It was the first major building to be restored after the attacks and was heralded as a sign of renewal. The Winter Garden was built in 1988 as the centerpiece of the World Financial Center, a collection of corporate towers north of Battery Park City. The magical space, nearly as large as the concourse of Grand Central Station, hosts concerts, dance performances, and art exhibits.*

Above: *Built a century apart, City Hall (1811), on the left, and the Woolworth Building (1913), on the right, are two architectural masterpieces of Lower Manhattan. Two centuries of development can be seen in the surrounding area. The Woolworth, named for the five-and-dime-store king who thought much bigger than nickels and dimes, was the world's tallest skyscraper for the first seventeen years of its life. The architect, Cass Gilbert, combined the Gothic style with modern technology, covering the steel skeleton with pointed window arches and pinnacles to emphasize the soaring form. Dubbed the "Cathedral of Commerce" when it was built, it is also unique in the annals of commercial development. Woolworth paid $13 million in cash to build it, and his company retained ownership for eighty-five years before selling it in 1998 for $155 million. Woolworth stores, once ubiquitous in small-town America, have disappeared, but the Woolworth Building remains an architectural legend.*

Left: *This snowy view through City Hall Park reveals three historic government buildings. On the far left, partly obscured by tree branches, is City Hall, built in 1811, and on the right is the tower of the Municipal Building, a twenty-five-story skyscraper completed in 1914 as expansion room for city offices. Between the two is the pyramidal crown of the Federal Courthouse, built in 1927. City Hall Park has gone through many changes in its 400-year history, from a communal pasture ground in the mid-seventeenth century to a poorhouse, prison, parade ground, and public execution site where the British hanged 250 American rebels during the Revolutionary War. It was also a place for historic gatherings in the nineteenth century, including Abraham Lincoln's funeral procession. The Victorian-style lampposts were installed in 1999 as part of a major park restoration.*

Right: *Seen through the lights of City Hall Park is the cupola atop City Hall. Nearly destroyed in a fire in the early 1900s, it has been restored several times, and its copper dome still holds a shining statue of Justice. Despite the destructive fire, severe deterioration, and calls for its demolition, City Hall is still the main seat of New York's government. The mayor and city council continue to conduct daily business here, as they have done for nearly two centuries.*

Left: This bull, with head lowered and nostrils flaring, ready to charge, was designed as a symbol of American resurgence after the stock market crash of 1987, but his angry stance could be seen as a reflection of more recent Wall Street problems. Despite the ups and downs of the market, the bull has been a hit with tourists ever since his surprise arrival. But city officials were not pleased when the 7,000-pound, eleven-foot-tall bronze sculpture appeared unannounced in front of the New York Stock Exchange one early morning in December 1989. The sculptor, Arturo Di Modica, called it a Christmas gift to the city. The police did not hesitate to look the gift horse—in this case a gift bull—in the mouth. They seized the sculpture and placed it in an impound lot. After a public outcry, it found a home here on Lower Broadway at Bowling Green Plaza, a small park two blocks south of the exchange.

Left: The dramatic angle of this unique aerial view can be seen as a map illuminating the heart of the financial district at Wall and Broad streets. The familiar neo-Roman facade of the stock exchange is on Broad Street. Wall Street is outlined by the vertical strip of yellow light shining on buildings on the south side of the street. The dark tower looming above on the right is 40 Wall Street, now called the Trump Building. It went up in 1930 in a race with the Chrysler Building to become the world's tallest building, but lost by 121 feet.

Above: The Roman temple facade of the 1903 New York Stock Exchange, with its monumental Corinthian columns, was part of the neoclassical trend sweeping the nation at the start of the twentieth century. The pediment contains an allegorical collection of figures representing "Integrity Protecting the Rights of Man." Over time, the figures deteriorated so badly that their stone was replaced with sheet metal. The work was done in secret, perhaps because it might have implied a state of crumbling integrity. The New York Stock Exchange officially dates to 1817, when formal rules and a constitution were adopted. The organization moved ten times before establishing its first base of operations here on Broad and Wall in 1865.

Left: *The statue of George Washington commemorates the spot—although not the actual building—where he took the oath of office as the first U.S. president in 1789. The original building was erected here at Wall and Broad streets in 1700 as the seat of the British colonial government. It became a key site for historic events in the years leading to the Revolution, notably in 1765 when the Stamp Act Congress proclaimed, "No taxation without representation." It was renamed Federal Hall after the American victory, and was the place where Congress enacted the Bill of Rights. Demolished in 1812, it was replaced in 1842 by this magnificent Greek Revival building. On September 16, 1920, a bomb hidden in a horse-drawn cart exploded in front of the building, killing forty people and wounding hundreds more. The building and Washington's statue weathered the attack without a scratch. On September 6, 2002, members of Congress met at Federal Hall, four blocks from ground zero, as a symbolic show of support for a city still recovering from the attacks of September 11, 2001.*

Right: *This is the third Trinity Church to stand here on Broadway at the head of Wall Street. The British colonial government built the first one in 1698. The church had an unlikely parishioner in the pirate captain William Kidd, who provided the block and tackle for hoisting the building stones. Kidd was a welcome figure in New York at the time, since English governors and wealthy New Yorkers often financed the pirate's lucrative raids on European ships and smuggled the loot back into the city. Both Kidd and the church came to unfortunate ends. He died on an English gallows in 1701, and the church burned in a citywide fire in 1776, likely set by American rebels at the start of the British occupation. The second version was built in 1790 but was demolished in 1839 because of structural problems. The present church, completed in 1846, is a Gothic Revival masterpiece by Richard Upjohn.*

Left: *Known by many names, and none of them well known, Wall Street Tower is nonetheless one of the most distinctive Art Deco towers in the canyons of Wall Street. It was built in 1932 as the Cities Service Building at 70 Pine Street, but was renamed the 60 Wall Street Tower when a bridge was built to that parallel street. The American International Group renamed it in the 1970s, but after its recent financial travails, AIG has been looking for another buyer, and the name may soon change again. Rising 950 feet, the slender building is amazingly squeezed onto a tiny footprint between narrow streets. The site is so small that double-decker elevators were built to serve two floors at a time and save the space of multiple elevator shafts. It was the last of the Jazz Age skyscrapers, and its Art Deco details make it a favorite of architectural buffs. The brightly lit pinnacle has a glass-enclosed observation deck (unfortunately closed to the public) that was outfitted inside with furniture designed by Le Corbusier and Marcel Breuer. The glass-faced buildings on the left are the more modern headquarters of two major banks, Marine Midland and Chase Manhattan.*

Right: *When this grand edifice opened in 1907, the only American Indians around were a few depicted in some of the building's sculptures. Created as the U.S. Customs House but now housing a branch of the Smithsonian National Museum of the American Indian, the magnificent structure presented a glorified view of New York history. It stands at the foot of Broadway, facing Bowling Green, then the center of New York's lucrative shipping empire. Its architect, Cass Gilbert, was little known at the time but would go on to design the nearby Woolworth Building and the Supreme Court Building in Washington, D.C. After shipping through the Port of New York declined, U.S. Customs moved in 1973 to smaller quarters in the newly built World Trade Center a few blocks away. Empty for years, the old building eventually took in new tenants. The upper floors became offices for the U.S. Bankruptcy Court, an ironic change in the building's preoccupation from wealth to debt. The main floor houses a vast collection of Indian artifacts assembled by New Yorker George Heye in the first half of the twentieth century.*

Right: *Looking south, this view takes in the Manhattan Bridge (foreground) and the Brooklyn Bridge. On the night the Brooklyn Bridge opened, May 24, 1883, a string of seventy lamps on the bridge were illuminated one by one, creating an arc of light across the river—a fantastic show no one had ever seen before. Lanterns were hung on the ship riggings lining the waterfront, and a few newly electrified buildings also joined the celebration. Today, the city's blaze of light outshines both bridges, but their silhouettes are a grace note along the skyline. The scene also includes Pier 17, outlined with lights at the base of the Brooklyn Bridge. The balconies on this three-story pier afford a seagull's view of the bridge, the river, and the occasional passing ship. In the skyline just above the pier is the illuminated pinnacle of the former Cities Service Building, the tallest tower on Wall Street, shown on page 36.*

Above: *Of the six bridges spanning the East River from Manhattan, these two are the best known. In this view toward Brooklyn, the Brooklyn Bridge (foreground) is unmistakable by the distinctive pointed arches of its massive stone towers. Older than the old piers in this photo, the bridge opened in 1883 as the first—and much celebrated— crossing over the river. An engineering wonder in its day, its nearly 1,600-foot span made it the longest suspension bridge in the world, twice the length of any bridge at the time. Its total length is more than 6,000 feet. It would take another two decades before a second bridge, the Williamsburg (not shown), crossed the river in 1903 with a longer span. The Manhattan Bridge (seen here in the background) followed in 1909 with decorative steel towers and a span slightly shorter than that of the Brooklyn Bridge. Tens of thousands of vehicles cross the bridges daily, in six lanes of traffic on the Brooklyn and seven on the Manhattan. The Manhattan also carries four subway lines and 320,000 mass-transit riders a day.*

Right: *There are many gateways to Manhattan, but the most romantic is the Brooklyn Bridge, particularly at night. Its monolithic stone towers connected by powerful cables and an airy web of steel are a thing of beauty. An inspiration to generations of artists, it was also the greatest architectural achievement of its day. Its towers rose higher and plunged deeper than any before them. The one seen here was the most difficult to build. Workers had to dig nearly eighty feet under the river to reach a stable foundation for the Manhattan tower, almost twice the depth needed for the Brooklyn tower. They toiled in huge, airtight shafts and the changing air pressure often caused painful cases of the bends—or even death. When the bridge opened in 1883 after fourteen years of construction, it was hailed as a wonder of the world. The tall building to the left of the bridge is the seventy-six-story Beekman Tower. Shown here under construction, it was designed by Frank Gehry and will wear a crinkled stainless-steel skin when completed. A few blocks from ground zero and Wall Street, the shimmering tower—New York's tallest residential building—will add a new dimension to the skyline.*

Below: *While many of Manhattan's ethnic neighborhoods lost their color and character in the urban renewal projects of the 1960s, Chinatown has held on for the most part and grown even larger. Like most of the Lower East Side, it got its share of new public housing. Chinatown's largest development—called Confucius Plaza— was built in 1976 on more than six acres near the Manhattan Bridge, and provided much-needed relief from overcrowded tenements. At the same time, the continuing flow of Chinese immigrants expanded the neighborhood, making inroads into the adjacent Little Italy and formerly Eastern European strongholds. Vibrant restaurants and food shops like this one draw people from all over the city and preserve Chinatown's distinctive flavor.*

Right: *From a few sailors and merchants working the trade between China and the United States in the mid-eighteenth century, New York's Chinatown has grown to become the most populous Chinese community in the Western Hemisphere. It began as a tiny enclave in Manhattan's Lower East Side known as "the bachelor society" because American immigration laws prevented most men from bringing their wives and families to join them. It was not until 1943 when President Franklin Roosevelt signed a measure repealing the Chinese Exclusion Act of 1882 that Chinese were allowed to become U.S. citizens. However, quotas for Chinese immigration remained low until they were abolished in 1965. Today, Manhattan's Chinatown has spread throughout the Lower East Side to other large enclaves in Brooklyn and Queens. While most residents are Chinese, the population has become more diverse since the 1980s, including immigrants from other Asian countries and Latin America.*

Left: *The nighttime scene looks quiet in the courthouses gathered around Foley Square, but more than likely, people were still working in the police headquarters, the low, square building in the top right corner. Established in 1845, the New York City Police Department is the largest police force in the country. The headquarters building, One Police Plaza, contains every type of law-enforcement and investigation activity, including the emergency command center, once located at the World Trade Center. The hexagonal building in the foreground is the New York State Supreme Court Building, built in 1927 with a commanding classical facade (shown above). Next to it is the United States Courthouse, a 1936 Classical Revival skyscraper, the last building designed by Cass Gilbert, architect of the nearby Woolworth Building and U.S. Customs House. It stands in front of two modern federal courthouses (center) that were added to handle the ever-increasing complexity of U.S. legal affairs.*

Above: *Often called the "Law and Order Steps," this 100-foot-wide flight is a familiar sight to viewers of the long-running television series. It also was the setting for a dramatic scene from the first Godfather film, in which a mob boss struck by gunfire plunges down the steps. New York's judicial system was once contained along with the legislature in nearby City Hall, but is now spread across the five boroughs. This courthouse, built in 1927 for the New York County Court, is now the home of the New York State Supreme Court. While plans were taking shape in the 1920s for masterpieces like the Chrysler Building and other Art Deco skyscrapers, classical architecture was still very much in order for the courts. Three huge statues representing Law, Truth, and Equity stand atop the 140-foot-long pediment.*

Left: Cars coming off the Manhattan Bridge pass this monumental bank on the Bowery and Canal Street as they enter Manhattan. Built in 1924, it faces the bridge colonnade across the street and serves as a classical counterpoise to that imposing structure (above). An elevated subway line once rose above the Bowery, and the bank was built high enough and capped with a dome to be seen above it. From the mid-nineteenth century until the Art Deco age of the 1930s, classical architecture was de rigueur for banks, and this splendid building was well within that dignified tradition. While several others have been converted to new uses, it has continued as a bank. Built as the Citizens Savings Bank, it is now a branch of HSBC, the Hongkong and Shanghai Banking Corporation, an appropriate institution for this Chinatown location. The HSBC signs, however, are no match for the historic building.

Above: Called the Court of Honor when it opened in 1912, this triumphal entrance to the Manhattan Bridge was designed by Carrere and Hastings, the architects who were working at the same time on the New York Public Library (1911). Both structures are impressive monuments of classical design, but this one was soon overwhelmed by traffic as cars, trucks, and buses took over the city's streets. It also became a portal in the early twentieth century for immigrants moving from tenements to slightly better quarters in Brooklyn. Today, the Brooklyn side is a trendy enclave known as DUMBO, or "down under the Manhattan Bridge overpass."

Above: *This neighborhood is on Manhattan's lower west side, but no one calls it that anymore. Tribeca, an acronym for "Triangle Beneath Canal Street," took hold in the 1980s when actor Robert De Niro established the Tribeca Film Center. The area, a wedge of old industrial buildings like the one in the foreground, provided ample, affordable space for independent film studios and a large cast of actors, writers, directors, editors, and the like who moved in nearby. The creative types gave the neighborhood a fashionable reputation and, as always,*

developers followed the trend. The tower pictured here is Trump SoHo, a forty-six-story hotel that opened in 2010. The building is actually a few blocks west of SoHo, or South of Houston, another formerly industrial and now übertrendy neighborhood. Even the pioneering actors have gotten into the development act. De Niro and his son Raphael are partners in Tribeca's Greenwich Hotel, opened in 2008. Raphael is also a real-estate broker for a new loft building, the Tribeca Fairchild, from which this photo was taken.

Right: *Appropriately known as the "Tower of Light," this twenty-six-story structure became the crowning glory of the Consolidated Edison Company in 1926, the year it controlled virtually all of the city's light and power franchises. Like so many people who achieved success in New York City, Thomas Edison, inventor of the first working electric lightbulb, was not shy of taking on the competition. This building began as the home of the gas companies that had merged to confront the spread of electricity. They eventually joined Edison to become today's powerhouse known as ConEd. Built in*

stages, the building covers an entire block on Irving Place between Fourteenth and Fifteenth streets near Union Square. Henry Hardenbergh, the architect of the Plaza Hotel and the Dakota Apartments, designed the first sections, and Warren and Wetmore, architects of Grand Central Station, designed the tower. In the lower left corner is the steeple of Grace Church on Sixth Avenue and Eleventh Street in Greenwich Village. It was designed by James Renwick in 1846, years before he began to create St. Patrick's Cathedral in 1858.

Above: An icon of Greenwich Village, the Washington Square Arch was built at the foot of Fifth Avenue in 1895. It followed a wooden original built in 1889 to commemorate the centennial of George Washington's inauguration as the nation's first president. It was so popular that the public paid for the marble version, created by Stanford White of the prominent architectural firm McKim, Mead, and White. The arch stands at the northern edge of Washington Square Park, once a pauper's cemetery and later a military parade ground. Henry James was born around the corner from Washington Square in 1843 and borrowed its name for one of his most famous novels. Edward Hopper lived in a walk-up flat facing the square from 1913 to 1967, and painted views of it from his window. Today the park is a popular gathering place for students from the surrounding New York University campus. Soapbox orators can often be heard against a background of impromptu folk, rock, and rap music. Directly opposite the arch is NYU's Bobst Library, designed by Philip Johnson in 1972, and the Judson Memorial Church and tower, White's eclectic architectural creation of 1890.

Top left: *Anthony Bleecker, who deeded his family farmland to the city in 1808, would never recognize Bleecker Street today. Nightclubs and restaurants line this Greenwich Village street from its eastern end at the Bowery, where the famous CBGB club pumped out hard rock, to the legendary Village Gate and Bitter End in the heart of the Village, where jazz, folk, and rock heroes from Duke Ellington to Pete Seeger to Patti Smith once played. This brightly lit corner is at Bleecker and Sixth Avenue, a few blocks from Washington Square Park.*

Bottom left: *Jimi Hendrix and Bob Dylan were rocking here in the 1960s, or actually just next door at the club's original location on MacDougal Street. Café Wha?, a name that conveyed the anything-goes atmosphere of the era, was also a regular hangout for the Beat poet Allen Ginsberg and for comedians Woody Allen, Lenny Bruce, Richard Pryor, and many others. MacDougal Street has a long history of intellectual hipsters and creative performers. Not far from Café Wha?, Eugene O'Neil staged his first play in 1918 at MacDougal Street's Provincetown Playhouse, the inspiration for little theaters and cutting-edge dramas that would sprout up across the country. O'Neil found lots of material for his plays at MacDougal Street bars.*

Right: *Longshoremen, labor organizers, socialists, writers, and bohemians of every stripe have pulled up to the bar in this Greenwich Village watering hole a few blocks from the Hudson River. New York Magazine called it the "nostalgic high temple of the Alcoholic Artist," and it has the tales to prove it. Jack Kerouac, a frequent customer who lived nearby on West Eleventh Street, was reportedly bounced from the establishment more than once. But its best-known patron was the Welsh poet and writer Dylan Thomas, who drank here on a regular basis in the 1950s and spent his last night at the bar before dying a few days later on November 9, 1953. The building dates to 1880 and is one of the few remaining wooden structures in Manhattan. Nestled within the nineteenth-century row houses of the West Village, its lights still beckon.*

Above: *The Christopher Street subway station, opened in 1918, is the gateway to the West Village, known for its artists, actors, poets, and free spirits of all kinds. E. E. Cummings, Yoko Ono, Philip Seymour Hoffman, and many others lived or still live on Christopher Street, the oldest street in this neighborhood. In the early 1800s, Greenwich Village residents convinced city officials to exempt their crooked colonial lanes from the new rigid street grid imposed on the rest of Manhattan. As a result, many Village streets are at odd angles to each other, winding along their* own way. In 1961 local resident Jane Jacobs, author of The Death and Life of Great American Cities, led a group that stopped urban-renewal advocates from demolishing a swath of the neighborhood, including many homes on Christopher Street. In 1969 Christopher Street's Stonewall Inn became the birthplace of the gay liberation movement when its patrons rioted against police arrests. The Village Cigars store is the first thing the main character sees when he gets off the subway in the 1976 coming-of-age film Next Stop, Greenwich Village.

Right: *Located in the Ladies Mile Historic District, this huge emporium, one of many large department stores built in the nineteenth century, is no longer just for ladies. It is now part of a new shopping district that carries everything from sports equipment to the latest fashions. The district covers more than a dozen blocks between Union and Madison squares from Park Avenue South to just west of Sixth Avenue. It includes a stretch of Broadway where this imposing building, the ABC Carpet and Home Store, offers trendy home furnishings and "the world's largest collection of* carpets and rugs." Department stores aimed at luring women shoppers began in the mid-nineteenth century when such major retailers as Lord & Taylor and B. Altman built palatial marble and cast-iron showplaces along Broadway and Sixth Avenue. After these companies moved uptown, the area was rediscovered in the 1980s by architects, photographers, advertising firms, and other cutting-edge businesses. They soon attracted restaurants, fashionable boutiques, and national merchandising chains that restored the architecturally distinctive buildings.

Right: *Three decades before the Empire State and Chrysler buildings rose on the skyline, the Flatiron Building was New York's first skyscraper icon. Built in 1903 on a traffic island surrounded by Fifth Avenue, Broadway, and Twenty-third Street, it fills its triangular site and still appears much taller than its twenty-three stories. The apex of the triangle is only six feet wide, and from the side, the building looks like a single thick wall. Head-on, it looks like an approaching locomotive. It was originally called the Fuller Building, but in the early 1900s, it seemed to resemble a household flatiron, and the name stuck. It may not look like a skyscraper today, but under its brick and terra-cotta facade the Flatiron is a modern slab, a radical architectural form in its day. The facade undulates over bay windows that project out from both sides of the wedge. The ripple effect makes the building shimmer in the changing light, as though its walls were the sails of a giant ship making its way up the avenue.*

Left: The stylized model of the Empire State Building projecting from its roof makes it clear that this is a New York City diner. It even has a Manhattan attitude and calls itself the "hippest diner on earth." While there are diners throughout the city, this is a 1940s Art Deco original. Its home is on Tenth Avenue and West Twenty-second Street in Chelsea, a neighborhood that was once simply working-class but which is now considered hip. But whatever the neighborhood's reputation, the diner has always attracted celebrities, from Babe Ruth to Bruce Springsteen. The diner's late-night hours bring in customers from every walk of life, from cab drivers to politicians and popular entertainers. Its motto is "Everyone eats here sooner or later." Its atmospheric interior has also been the setting for many movies and television shows, including Men in Black II, Home Alone II, Law and Order, and the opening credits from Saturday Night Live. But all that may change. The diner's operators for the past thirty years lost their lease and left the diner in May 2010. While they look for another location, New Yorkers will be waiting to see if the new restaurateurs live up to the Empire Diner legend.

Above and following pages: The Empire State Building—the inspiration for this classic New York diner.

Left: *The first light to shine from the top of the Empire State Building was a searchlight beacon in November 1932, a signal that Franklin D. Roosevelt had been elected president. Four beacons installed in 1956 revolved in synchronization, one revolution per minute. The building became a nighttime landmark when a new series of floodlights illuminated the top thirty floors in April 1964 to celebrate the opening of the New York World's Fair. Colored lighting was introduced in 1976, with red, white, and blue lights for the bicentennial. White and blue lights first flashed on October 12, 1977, to announce that the Yankees had won the World Series. Today, more than a thousand fluorescent tubes light up the mast in a rainbow of changing colors—such as green for St. Patrick's Day, as shown on page 55. The lights of Times Square can be seen on the left.*

Above and right: *Rowland Hussey Macy, a former whaler, began this legendary store as a dry-goods shop on Union Square in 1858 but did not live to see it rise to its full glory. The innovative entrepreneurs Isidor and Nathan Strauss, who once sold china in the original store, moved the business uptown to this huge building on Broadway and Thirty-fourth Street in 1905. Previously, this corner was the site of Oscar Hammerstein's Manhattan Opera House, which moved farther uptown to the new theater district on Forty-second Street and Broadway. Macy's big red sign covers a smaller building that the Strauss brothers had failed to acquire at first. Legend has it that the red star logo came from R. H. Macy's tattoo. The new building made Macy's the world's largest department store, but it may have to change its sign. A giant emporium opened in 2009 in South Korea is now claiming the title. Macy's is a particular favorite at Christmastime, as pictured at right, and was memorialized in the 1947 film Miracle on 34th Street as the place where the real Santa Claus hangs out. Although it is not the fanciest store in New York—many farther uptown have much higher price tags—Macy's is ensconced as a city icon and National Historic Landmark.*

Above: Libraries were a luxury only the rich could afford before this people's palace of books was built in 1911. Three of the city's largest private libraries came together in 1895 to contribute their collections and endowments for the New York Public Library. Andrew Carnegie provided most of the construction funds for the Beaux Arts building on Fifth Avenue and Forty-second Street, as he would do for many smaller libraries throughout the city. The Main Reading Room, seen here, is a majestic public space nearly two city blocks long. The long oak tables are lit by elegant bronze lamps under fifty-two-foot-high ceilings decorated with vibrant murals of billowing clouds. This is the core research center for a citywide library system of eighty-five neighborhood branches. Norman Mailer, Isaac Bashevis Singer, E. L. Doctorow, and many other New York–based literary figures and scholars gathered their information here. The Main Reading Room was restored in 1998 with a $15 million gift from members of the Rose family.

Left: *This stretch of Forty-second Street running alongside Bryant Park (right) was a dangerous place at night when drug dealers dominated the park in the 1970s. It is a beautiful and safe retreat today, so safe that the renovated restroom shown here has a diaper-changing table for babies. The classical building just above the restroom is the New York Public Library. The Chrysler dome shining at the eastern end of Forty-second Street is a graceful beam of light amid the wall of rectangular office buildings.*

Above: *Bryant Park was named in 1884 for the poet and editor William Cullen Bryant, a strong advocate for public parks. In 1844 he began a campaign to build Central Park, which began construction in 1858. Bryant Park's history dates even earlier to 1847, when it was called Reservoir Square for the reservoir once located next to it on the site of today's library. Reservoir Square had a brief period of fame when the Crystal Palace rose there in 1853. It was modeled on the one in London, but New York's grand exposition hall went up in flames in 1858. The park was reshaped in 1934 with a sunken central lawn surrounded by granite balustrades and London plane trees. But by the 1970s it had became a haven for drug dealers and the homeless. It was restored in the 1980s as this splendid midtown oasis. This view looks west toward office buildings on Sixth Avenue.*

Right and following pages: *Detail of the Chrysler dome.*

Left and right: *Like an Art Deco rocket ship that landed in New York, the Chrysler Building brought a vision of fantasy to the city skyline. Seventy-seven stories high, it also won an actual race to become the world's tallest tower in 1930. The architect, William Van Alen, was racing to outdo his former partner, Craig Severance, who was building a competing tower at 40 Wall Street. The architects kept increasing the number of floors and, at the last minute, Van Alen installed this 185-foot spire to surpass his rival by 121 feet. Van Alen worked closely with automobile magnate Walter Chrysler, and the building incorporates many design details found on cars. Layers of stainless steel covering the dome look like the rims of overlapping hubcaps. Gargoyles projecting from the building's corners could be gigantic hood ornaments. Criticized as ostentatious in its day, the Chrysler is loved today precisely for its flashy yet sophisticated style.*

Following pages: *Flamboyant Times Square is the ironic namesake of the New York Times, known as the "Gray Lady" for its disdain of flashy journalism. The subdued history of this famous center of New York glitter is hidden today behind the giant video screens that cover the original Times Tower (center). The newspaper ventured uptown to this relatively undeveloped area in 1904. The new building, dressed in Italian Renaissance terra-cotta, was a stately home for the paper, but it sowed the seeds of a flashier future. On New Year's Eve 1908, an illuminated ball was lowered from the tower at midnight, launching the city's famous tradition. The newspaper moved to another building in 1913, and in 1963 the Allied Chemical Company stripped off the terra-cotta dress and reclad the tower in concrete and marble belted by a moving sign of flashing headlines. The 1960s began an era of sleaze for Times Square, but in the 1990s the neighborhood cast off its squalid past with a wave of new investment. Times Tower is now surrounded by restored theaters, new office towers, and family attractions in an exuberant commercial celebration.*

Left: *The famous lights of Broadway burn brightest on West Forty-second Street, the heart of Times Square, just a block off Broadway. Today it is known as the "New Forty-second Street," signaling its rebirth from the bad old days of the 1970s, when it was plagued by drug dealers and adult entertainment. It came back to life in the 1990s with elegantly refurbished theaters and glittering new attractions. On the right is one that went through the greatest transformation, the AMC Empire Cineplex, originally the 1912 Empire Theater. It is one of Forty-second Street's architectural treasures, distinguished by an eighty-foot-wide terra-cotta facade and a triumphal arch window. One of the city's old vaudeville houses, it is where the comedy team of Bud Abbott and Lou Costello made their debut in 1935.*

Above: *At its nadir, Times Square flashed signs advertising adult films. Today it is all about family entertainment, and this fifteen-story-high sign is one of the main attractions. It towers above the Hershey's candy store that opened on Broadway and Forty-eighth Street in 2002. In the old days, when Times Square flaunted bad habits, one of its most famous signs was for Camel cigarettes—it began to blow steam-powered smoke rings in 1941 and kept puffing for the next twenty-five years. Now, the steam that rises here comes from a giant cup of Hershey's cocoa.*

Previous pages: *The brilliantly lit Times Tower may be the center of attention, but the building that embodies the glory days of Times Square is the one in the right foreground with the pyramid shape and illuminated globe. This is the Paramount Building (1927), where movie stars became famous in the 1930s and rock and roll exploded in the 1950s. Gary Cooper, Fred Astaire, Bing Crosby, and many other Hollywood stars were introduced at the palatial Paramount Theater. In the 1940s, Frank Sinatra played here to the screams of teenage bobby-soxers, but music took off in a whole new direction with the Allan Freed Rock and Roll Show. Freed was known as the "Father of Rock and Roll" because he was credited with coining the name. He showcased Elvis Presley and other legends of the era. The Beatles played here in 1964, one of the theater's last big-name acts. Today, the restored theater is home to the Hard Rock Cafe.*

Right: *This is the heart of Times Square, where Broadway, Seventh Avenue, Forty-second Street, and Forty-third Street cross. The original Times Tower (center) is surrounded by much bigger buildings added over the past decade. But the newest and most unlikely development is down in the square. Here, in the midst of the city's most frenetic traffic, a unique pedestrian mall was created in 2010 by banning cars from six blocks of the adjacent Broadway. Tourists and New Yorkers make good use of the picnic tables and folding chairs, even under the neon lights. The red dots on the right are café umbrellas.*

Left: *Times Square seems to generate its own blue-flame intensity at the core of the city. Although this part of Broadway is still known as the Great White Way, the name took hold not here but much farther downtown, on Lower Broadway from the Bowery to Grand Street in 1826, when that area was illuminated by 120 gas lamps. Previously lit by oil lamps, this was the start of the Broadway theater district that would reach Times Square by the time of World War I. In 1927–28, the electric marquees of seventy-six Broadway theaters twinkled with the names of 264 shows. The lights dimmed during the Great Depression and again during World War II when the area, flooded with servicemen on leave, became a haven for vice. The tide changed in the 1990s when new developments brought in a wave of towers ablaze with neon lights. The Great White Way is going green today, as all of the theater marquees have switched to energy-efficient lights.*

Left: *Elevated on a platform above Park Avenue, Grand Central Terminal's triumphal triple-arched facade is a grand gateway to the city. Opened in 1913, it was the second railroad terminal at Forty-second Street. The first, built in 1871, was then at the city's northern outskirts and critics complained that it was "neither grand nor central." The new terminal included both this magnificent building and a vast system of underground tracks covered by new streets and buildings. The immense project transformed the city's northern frontier into a midtown that would* become a new skyscraper district rivaling Lower Manhattan. *The huge building behind the terminal went up in 1963 and was called a "monstrous wet blanket" because it smothered views of Park Avenue. But Grand Central Terminal still stands out as a splendid landmark. The sculpture group and clock above the central arch, topped by the figure of Mercury astride an eagle, is as well known as the building itself. In front of the terminal is a statue of Cornelius Vanderbilt, who created the New York Central Railroad in 1863.*

Above: *After an eighty-year migration, this monumental eagle returned to Grand Central Terminal and found a new perch atop the canopy over the building's Lexington Avenue entrance. It was one of nearly a dozen iron eagles—all with thirteen-foot wingspans—adorning the facade of the first Grand Central Terminal, which stood at this site from 1871 to 1910. After the old terminal was demolished to make way for the current one built in 1913, the eagles were dispersed among private estates and institutions in New York State. This one was discovered amid a tangle* of bushes in a suburban backyard in Bronxville. *The owners donated it for the restoration of the current terminal in the 1990s. The top of the Chrysler Building can be seen on the right.*

Left: *Grand Central Terminal's main concourse, with its great arched windows and vaulted ceiling traced with starlit constellations, is one of the premier public spaces in the United States. But in the 1950s, with highways outpacing train service, the New York Central Railroad tried to demolish the building. When that failed, they proposed a tower above it that would have pierced this room with steel shafts. Preservationists, led by Jacqueline Kennedy Onassis, waged years of lawsuits that ultimately reached the U.S. Supreme Court, the first historic preservation battle to get that far, and finally secured landmark protection in 1978. After years of neglect, the grand space was beautifully restored in 1998. It continues to be a vibrant place for social interaction and an inspiration to the tens of thousands who pass through each day.*

Left: *The slender black tower in the center is the seventy-two-story Trump World Tower, said to be the world's tallest residential building when it opened on First Avenue and Forty-seventh Street in 2001. The East River and the borough of Queens are in the background. Neighbors complained that it would overwhelm the nearby United Nations Building. Like most of Donald Trump's big buildings, it went up amid controversy and lawsuits, but it went up all the same. In the river on the far left is Roosevelt Island and the illuminated ruin of an historic hospital (see page 138).*

Above: *Park Avenue is a fabled address that conjures up images of elegant penthouses—and there are many of these, to be sure. From this section north of Grand Central Terminal up to Ninety-sixth Street, the avenue runs through one of the city's wealthiest areas. But a much different history lies underground. Before the current terminal was built, this section was a dirty and dangerous expanse of open train yards, a death trap for working-class New Yorkers who lived along its borders. In addition to the terminal, which was completed in 1913, the railroad built an*

intricate system of underground tracks and covered them with these newly created streets. Developers purchased air rights from the railroad and built office towers, hotels, and apartment buildings, many of them connected to the terminal by underground passageways. This view looks south toward the Helmsley Building with its brightly lit crown. It was built in 1929 as the opulent headquarters of the New York Central Railroad.

Above and right: *Like a modern-day Roman Forum, the Lincoln Center, a collection of classically inspired buildings all clad in travertine marble, is a compendium of culture facing a public plaza. It covers sixteen acres of Manhattan's Upper West Side and houses a dozen arts institutions and organizations involved in every type of musical and theatrical performance. The focal point is the Metropolitan Opera House, whose Austrian crystal chandeliers shine through the monumentally arched windows. One of the more successful products of the urban renewal projects of the 1960s, the complex is the work of the leading architects of the day, including Philip Johnson, who designed the New York State Theater, seen here on the left. Johnson also designed the plaza, inlaid with spokes of marble encircling an illuminated fountain. The fountain has been a scenic backdrop for several movies, including The Producers, Moonstruck, and Ghost Busters. It was renovated in 2009 and now performs an even more spectacular water ballet, shooting sprays as high as forty feet with 475 gallons of water in the air. The long flight of steps leading to the plaza was also rebuilt to provide easier access from the street. The plaza was part of a $1.2 billion renovation for the Lincoln Center, including thirty improvement projects still in the works.*

THE PACKARD COLLECTION
5,000 years of Japanese art

PABLO BRONSTEIN

THE DRAWINGS OF
BRONZINO

VICTORIAN PHOTOCOLLAGE

Mastering the Art of Chinese Painting
Xie Zhiliu (1910–1997)

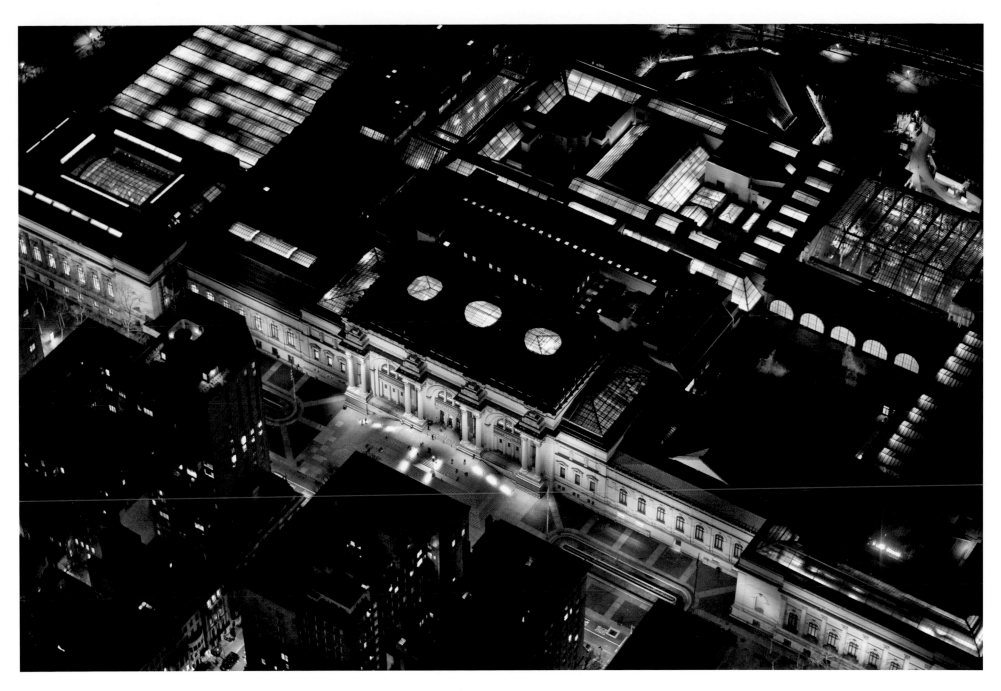

Left and above: At night, the Metropolitan Museum of Art's Greco-Roman entrance pavilion glows like an ancient temple. By day, the broad steps are one of the city's liveliest gathering places. The first wing of this palatial museum opened in 1880 at Fifth Avenue and Eightieth Street on the eastern edge of Central Park. The modest beginning, a Gothic Revival building created by Culvert Vaux, one of the park's designers, was engulfed in a century-long series of classical additions unrivaled by any museum in America. Although park advocates opposed the encroachment on green space, the museum's expansive collections and blockbuster exhibits of major artists has made it one of the city's greatest attractions. Its size and popularity would amaze some of the museum's nineteenth-century founders who feared that its location might be too remote from the city's center to attract visitors. Extending over four blocks to Eighty-fourth Street and deeper into the park, it is the Versailles of art museums and houses the most comprehensive art collection in the Western world.

Left: *Before the fifty-story Worldwide Plaza tower was built on West Forty-ninth Street in 1989, Irish gangs ruled the neighborhood. Real-estate agents call the area West Midtown, but it was better known as Hell's Kitchen, a mix of warehouses and tenements that became a breeding ground for crime. In the nineteenth century, poor Irish immigrants settled here in shantytowns and worked on the docks along the nearby Hudson River. The area was the setting for West Side Story, the Broadway musical and film that depicted battles between rival Irish, Italian, and Puerto Rican gangs here in the 1950s. Federal convictions in the 1980s ended the reign of the Westies, the most violent Irish gang. The tower, part of a three-building commercial and residential complex, includes several theaters and has attracted young and affluent professionals and actors.*

Right: *The GE Building rises from the center of Rockefeller Center, but its place was originally reserved for the Metropolitan Opera. When the opera pulled out, the project was renamed Radio City, and John D. Rockefeller gave the starring role to General Electric as a center for its radio networks, RCA and NBC. The tower was called the RCA Building for many years, but RCA eventually disappeared in corporate mergers as GE's empire changed from radio to television. The building is also known as 30 Rockefeller Center and is the fictional setting of the popular TV show 30 Rock. Some of the scenes are filmed in NBC's television studios in the building. At the very top of the seventy-story building is an observation deck, called Top of the Rock, which provides 360-degree views of New York. At its base is the famous Rockefeller Center ice-skating rink.*

Left and right: *Rising in the midst of Rockefeller Center, the slender, seventy-story GE Building had a radically new form for its day. It rose in 1933 not from a base, as did the Empire State and Chrysler buildings just a few years earlier, but directly from the street as a slab of form-fitting limestone. The streamlined building is the punctuation point for a coordinated collection of nearly twenty office towers, theaters, and restaurants, all connected to a public plaza and underground shopping complex. Covering several blocks in midtown Manhattan, it was built during the worst years of the Depression, sustained by Rockefeller funds.*

Left: *When construction of St. Patrick's Cathedral began in 1858, its site was a raw outpost chosen for its affordability. Today, St. Patrick's occupies a priceless piece of midtown Manhattan real estate, a full block between Madison and Fifth avenues and Fiftieth and Fifty-first streets, opposite Rockefeller Center (seen here on the right). Thousands of Irish Catholics, the city's largest immigrant group at the time, contributed their pennies to build the cathedral. Two years after the foundation was laid, construction was interrupted by the Civil War and did not resume until 1869. The cathedral opened in 1879, but its twin spires, each 330 feet high from street level, were not completed until 1888. With seating for 2,200 people, it is the largest Catholic cathedral in the United States.*

Top right: *The cathedral's neo-Gothic form, surrounded by the archbishop's house and rectory, is a commanding presence on its Madison Avenue frontage. The GE Tower at Rockefeller Center can be seen in the left background. In the right background is the glass-walled Olympic Tower, a luxury mix of apartments and offices that arrived in 1976, an eager neighbor for this prime location.*

Bottom right: *The vast interior of the cathedral includes intimate spaces such as this side altar. St. Patrick's has held requiem masses for such notable New Yorkers as Robert F. Kennedy and Babe Ruth. A special memorial mass was held in 1987 for Andy Warhol, who rose to fame and died in New York. Funerals were also held for many of the police officers and firefighters who perished in the fall of the World Trade Center in 2001.*

Previous pages: *The thin slab of the United Nations Secretariat Building can be seen in the left foreground on the riverfront. Completed in 1953, the 544-foot-high tower is a pure rectangle, 287 feet wide and only 72 feet thick. To the right of the United Nations, the swath of buildings in the foreground are part of the Upper East Side, New York's most affluent neighborhood, extending from Fifty-ninth to Ninety-sixth Street, between the East River and Central Park. Several distinctive skyscrapers can be seen in this panoramic view, which reaches to Manhattan's Hudson River shore and New Jersey in the background. On the far right is the slanted roof of the Citicorp Tower. The spires of the Empire State Building and Chrysler Building rise above the Manhattan skyline in the center of the photo. On the left are two lower, lighted spires. The taller one is the Metropolitan Life Tower and the shorter one is the New York Life Building.*

Right: *In this age of 3-D IMAX movie screens, it is hard to imagine the attraction of a theater called Radio City. But it was an exciting concept when this grand music hall opened in midtown Manhattan in 1932. Radio City was the original name for Rockefeller Center, and the music hall was just one building in that Art Deco metropolis. With 6,200 seats, the hall was the largest theater in the world. It began as a vaudeville stage and soon switched to movies, premiering King Kong in 1933, in combination with live performances by the dancing Rockettes. It was a top showplace for family entertainment in the 1950s, but fell on hard times in the 1970s. Now beautifully restored, its striking Art Deco interior is once again a premier venue for live concerts. Many events that are held here, like the MTV Video Awards, are televised, an unheard-of phenomenon in Radio City's early days. The Rockettes still perform each year in their Radio City Christmas Spectacular. During the rest of the year, a diverse cast of performers, from Cirque du Soleil to Lady Gaga, are onstage.*

Right: *This view of eastern midtown Manhattan includes two famous corporate towers expressed in different forms of twentieth-century architecture. The newer and taller one, the Citicorp Tower (1977), is mostly blocked by another building but is unmistakable by the steep slant of its silver-skinned roof. The slanted crown contains a 400-ton mass of concrete that counters the sway of the seventy-seven-story tower. Facing south, the slope was designed to be a solar collector to supplement the building's tremendous use of energy. But in those early days of environmental technology, it was determined that the cost was not worth the investment. The black, rectangular tower to the right is the Seagram Building (1958), the only work in New York City by the modernist master Ludwig Mies van der Rohe, a principal founder of the spare International Style of the 1920s. Although it looks black, the thirty-eight-story building is a shaft of bronze and glass. It was built to celebrate the centennial of the Seagram Company.*

Right: *The banners hanging above the entrance to the Museum of Modern Art spell the acronym that has become its affectionately fitting nickname. The MoMA is the mother of all contemporary art museums. It has inspired and nurtured other collections and cultivated America's perception of modern art. Like many of the city's cultural institutions, it got its start with the Rockefeller family, appropriately in this case by a matriarch, Abby Aldrich Rockefeller. She held the first exhibit in modest quarters in 1929, a time when modern art was widely dismissed by the public. Although her husband, John D. Rockefeller Jr., disapproved of modern art, she eventually convinced him to donate the land for the museum's current location on East Fifty-third Street off Fifth Avenue, once the site of a Rockefeller townhouse. The International Style building, with its austere facade of marble and glass, opened to the public in 1939. It gained worldwide prominence with its Pablo Picasso retrospective of 1939–40, and has also helped make many other modern artists household names. Expanded several times, most recently in 2004, it holds one of the largest collections of modern Western masterpieces.*

Above: The name Carnegie Hall has spelled success for thousands of musical figures—from Tchaikovsky to the Rolling Stones—who have performed in this famous concert hall since its opening in 1891. It also reflects its enormously successful benefactor, Andrew Carnegie, who paid a million dollars to build the magnificent neo-Renaissance building known for its marvelous acoustics. In its opening year, the Polish pianist Jan Ignace Paderewski made his American debut at the hall, followed by virtually every major classical, jazz, folk, and rock musician over the next century. Once home to the New York Philharmonic, it was scheduled for demolition in the 1960s when the orchestra moved to the newly built Lincoln Center. A coalition of musicians, politicians, and civic figures led by violinist Isaac Stern saved Carnegie Hall. It became a National Historic Landmark in 1964, and was completely restored to its original glory in the 1980s. Carnegie Hall Tower, a sixty-story building constructed next door on a lot originally acquired by Andrew Carnegie in 1903, provides the revenue to keep the music playing in the historic hall.

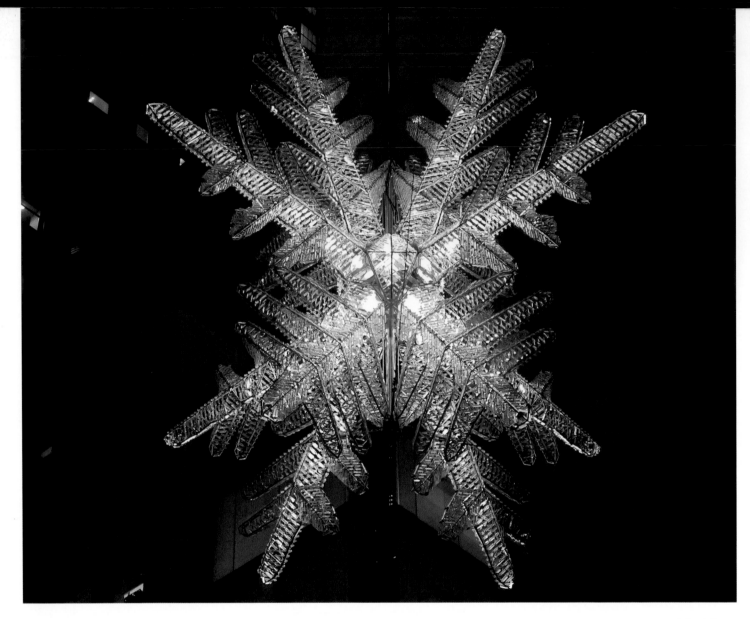

Above: *A giant snowflake comprised of 16,000 Baccarat crystals has been an iconic symbol of the New York holiday season for more than twenty years. Twenty-eight feet high and twenty-three feet in diameter, the snowflake, which weighs 3,300 pounds, is hung each year above the heart of the city's famous shopping center on Fifth Avenue and Fifty-seventh Street. In 2002 it was dedicated to the U.S. Fund for UNICEF, the United Nations International Children's Emergency Fund. The annual lighting ceremony kicks off a series of fund-raisers for the organization.*

Right: *The Trump Tower, the black building on the left with ascending rows of lit trees, arrived on this stylish section of Fifth Avenue in 1983. Critics complained that the glass tower did not belong on this quietly elegant stretch of low-rise, limestone-clad stores. It displaced the Art Deco department store Bonwit Teller, and opponents warned that it would do further harm by clashing with other Fifth Avenue doyens such as Tiffany's next door, on the left. But this location, in the midst of the city's most famous shopping district, just a block south of the Plaza Hotel and Central Park, was a developer's dream. The sleek tower was one of the first New York skyscrapers to burst out of its glass box. It has a taut glass skin pleated in folds over the length of its sixty-eight floors. The lower stories are an inverted pyramid of glass cubes supporting a small forest of trees. More glass towers would follow Trump here, bringing more tourists and more architectural critiques.*

Above: *Despite its name, the Brooklyn Diner is in Manhattan. The irony is not lost on generations of Brooklynites who once felt like second-class citizens in the big city. Now Brooklyn has retro appeal and the diner is awash with the borough's memorabilia. The diner proved so popular that it now occupies two prime Manhattan locations, one in Times Square and this one near Carnegie Hall.*

Right: *The transparent glass cube on the left is the entrance to the Apple Computer Store, the newest kid on the block in this prime section of Fifth Avenue shopping. It is surrounded by commercial royalty that has reigned on this corner of Fifth Avenue and Fifty-eighth Street for the better part of the last century. Directly behind the cube is the world-famous jewelry store Tiffany's, which has been on this corner since 1940. In the center is Manhattan's premier women's department store, Bergdorf-Goodman, opened in 1928, and on the far right is the Plaza Hotel, which opened in 1907. The glowing building behind Bergdorf's actually wears a shining crown and, in fact, is the Crown Building. It was built in 1921, and in 1929 its twelfth floor housed the first galleries of the Museum of Modern Art. The Apple Store opened underground in 2006 and, unlike its older retail neighbors, stays open twenty-four hours a day, every day. A glass elevator takes customers beneath the surface. The fountain in the foreground is one of two reflecting pools in the General Motors Plaza.*

Above and right: *Ever since the Plaza Hotel opened in 1907, a stream of famous people has passed through its grand entrance. Robber barons and royalty once rubbed shoulders in the gilded dining rooms, and F. Scott Fitzgerald made the Oak Bar his favorite watering hole in the 1920s. While working on the ultramodern Guggenheim Museum in the 1950s, Frank Lloyd Wright chose the Plaza Hotel's old-world charm for his regular lodging. The Beatles also stayed here on their first visit to* New York City in 1964. The Plaza became the preeminent premises for American tycoons and visiting royalty. The site itself is ideal; few New York buildings enjoy as much or as scenic open space. Framed by Central Park and the Grand Army Plaza, the hotel stands out like a giant French château and maintains its dignity even with the monolithic glass tower looming over it. An actual château, or at least an American version of one, was once a close neighbor. Built for Cornelius Vanderbilt II, it *was replaced in 1928 by Bergdorf-Goodman (far left of the main image), a fashionable women's clothing store. Donald Trump owned the hotel for a few years in the 1980s but sold it at a loss after an expensive divorce settlement with his first wife, who had redecorated most of the rooms. In 2007, its centennial year, a new group of developers reopened the hotel with a combination of renovated hotel rooms and multimillion-dollar apartments.*

Right: *The star of this west midtown view is not the black slab in the center, which appears taller than it actually is, but the tower flooded with light just to the left. Completed in 2006, the forty-two-story Hearst Tower realized a plan envisioned by William Randolph Hearst in 1928, the year he completed a six-story base on this site to house his publishing empire and anticipated that a tower would one day rise above it. However, the Great Depression ended that dream. Seven decades later, the British architect Sir Norman Foster was commissioned to design the tower, and it began construction despite another catastrophe. It was the first New York skyscraper to break ground after September 11, 2001. The triangular framing gives the tower a unique appearance, particularly when light shines through its transparent glass walls. The unusual structure required less steel than conventional towers and also consumes less energy. The building is on Eighth Avenue and Fifty-seventh Street, two blocks south of Columbus Circle, which is partially visible on the right. The Hudson River can be seen in the background.*

Left: *The Time Warner Center, the two towers with brightly lit tops, was built in 2004 after years of contention about big development at this site opposite Central Park. (The park's Fifty-ninth Street entrance is at the top left, facing Columbus Circle at the base of the towers.) After several years of trying, a previous developer had withdrawn his proposal in the face of strong opposition that it would overshadow the park. One of the most influential opponents was Jacqueline Kennedy Onassis, who led a long line of protesters in the park opening umbrellas in unison to symbolize the potential shadow. The space between the Time Warner buildings allows daylight as well as dramatic views of the sun when it passes between the towers, creating a modern-day Stonehenge. At 2.8 million square feet, the complex houses a vertical city of shops, restaurants, apartments, offices, a hotel, and concert halls. To the left of the towers is the Trump International Hotel and Tower, a retrofit of the Gulf and Western Building, which had been on the site since the 1960s.*

Right: *The nighttime lights swirling around Columbus Circle reflect New York's around-the-clock traffic patterns. This is one of Manhattan's busiest intersections, joining traffic heading in all directions. The view looks southward toward Broadway (left) and Eighth Avenue (right). On the far left is Fifty-ninth Street and the southwest corner of Central Park. The column in the center, topped with a statue of Christopher Columbus, was installed in 1892, the 400th anniversary of his landing in the New World. Even then, the circle was a hectic place surrounded by commercial buildings. By the early 1900s, subways would be running underground, with heavy automobile traffic circling above. For most of the twentieth century, Columbus Circle could not compete with the fashionable Fifth Avenue district across the park. But luxury arrived soon after the new millennium. The curved building on the far right is the high-end shopping center of the Time Warner Center. The smaller gray building between Broadway and Eighth Avenue is the new Museum of Art and Design, which opened in 2008.*

Above: *This view looks north toward Broadway (left) and Central Park West (right). On the right is the Fifty-ninth Street entrance to Central Park, marked by the Maine Monument, erected in 1913 to honor the American sailors who died in the explosion of the USS Maine during the Spanish-American War. The curved building on the far left is the Time Warner Center.*

Right: *At first glance, this looks like the huge Unisphere erected in Flushing Meadows Park in Queens for the 1964 World's Fair, but this isn't it. Donald Trump, a native of Queens, liked the Unisphere so much that he commissioned this smaller version to stand in front of the Trump International Hotel and Tower, which opened facing Columbus Circle in 1996. The international theme made it an appropriate site, or so he thought. But city officials did not agree. The problem was that Trump erected the globe on property controlled by the city and did so without an official permit. As in the case of the bronze bull that a sculptor delivered unannounced on Wall Street in 1989, the globe has taken root. City officials may grumble, but tourists love it.*

Right: *A project this big might have had a hard time fitting into Manhattan's tight street grid, particularly here, where several major thoroughfares and Central Park converge around Columbus Circle. But the architects of the Time Warner Center,* *completed in 2004, skillfully molded the buildings to fit within this jigsaw puzzle. The base of the building curves around Columbus Circle, and the sharp angles of the two towers carry the curve upward for fifty-five stories each.*

Right: *A mass of towers are piled up at the southeastern edge of Central Park along Fifth Avenue and Fifty-ninth Street, also known as Central Park South. When construction of the park began in 1859, few buildings could be seen here. By the time of the park's completion in 1873, mansions were rising along these southern borders. Over the years, the park became a magnet for bigger developments, pushing buildings up higher to take advantage of the irresistible views. Still a luxury residential neighborhood, this area is also packed with corporate office towers and elegant hotels. A few distinctive ones can be seen in the dense accumulation of buildings on the right. Bathed in bright light, the relatively low tower with the pointed top is the appropriately named Crown Building (1921). On the far right horizon is the slanted roof of the Citicorp Tower (1977). Just below it to the left is the Sony Building, a postmodern oddity by Philip Johnson with a crown like the top of a Chippendale dresser.*

Left: *Embraced by the glow of city lights, Central Park is a lush oasis even at night. Its forest of deep green treetops is a cushioning presence within a city of concrete and steel. This is a view of the park's southern edge, just a third of the park's 843 acres and its 26,000 trees. This section includes many of the park's most famous landmarks, including the Pond, Zoo, and Carousel. The pocket of soft light within the trees (right) reveals only one of the many attractions, the Wollman Skating Rink, open on this warm night for summertime activities. The view looks west from a Fifth Avenue apartment tower overlooking the park. The buildings on the left are on Central Park South, a street of elegant residences and hotels, including the famous Plaza Hotel on the far left. In the background is Central Park West with the lighted tops (center) of the twin-towered Time Warner Center.*

Left: *With music playing and the lights of the skyline as a backdrop, nighttime skating in Central Park is a romantic experience. Ice-skating has been a popular pastime in the park since 1858. Skaters began gliding over the park's frozen lake that winter, in the same year that park construction began. By 1950, the lake was considered unsafe for skating, so this artificial rink opened in 1951. Kate Wollman, a Kansas-born New Yorker, donated the funds for this rink, as well as for one in Brooklyn's Prospect Park. Measuring 214 by 175 feet, Central Park's Wollman Rink was the world's largest rink in its day. Today, as many as 4,000 ice-skaters use the rink on a daily basis. A children's amusement park takes over the rink in the summer season.*

Above: *Lushly green in the daytime, Central Park's most compelling feature at night is its intoxicating juxtaposition to the city skyline. The sprinkling of lights in the park is a delicate contrast to the surrounding explosion of building lights. This is the southern end of the park, where it meets the deepest sea of skyscrapers. Farther south, the Empire State Building's familiar tower can be seen in the center near the horizon. Within the park, the brightest patch of light is the Wollman Skating Rink. The largest expanse of darkness, in the right foreground, is the Sheep Meadow, where protesters gathered during the Vietnam War and where sunbathers and kite flyers now frolic.*

Left: *Seemingly poured over the lake, the Bow Bridge is an icon of Central Park. Built in 1862, it is one of three dozen bridges in the park, each one a unique design. Its span is exquisitely laced with Greek and Gothic details, but its graceful exterior hides an unusual foundation. The stone abutments rest on cannonballs, which act as movable bearings, allowing the cast-iron span to expand and contract in changing weather conditions. Looking west, this view includes the San Remo Apartment Towers, one of four twin-towered buildings on Central Park West, all built in the 1930s. A host of film stars and musical celebrities have lived in the San Remo's luxurious apartments, from Eddie Cantor and Rita Hayworth to Steven Spielberg, Dustin Hoffman, Demi Moore, and Bono.*

Above and right: *Inside one of Central Park's architectural treasures, the young people are playing a nighttime game of chamball (right), a combination of dodgeball and martial arts. Their arena is a gloriously decorated arcade connecting the park's tree-lined Mall to the famed Bethesda Terrace. The arcade was designed by Calvert Vaux, who together with Frederick Law Olmsted created the magnificent, 843-acre park. The vaulted ceiling is covered with 16,000 Minton tiles from England. Designed by Vaux's artistic assistant Jacob Wrey Mould, each tile is richly colored and glazed with intricate patterns reminiscent of those in the Alhambra in Spain. During the city's financial crisis of the 1970s, the park fell into serious disrepair; water seeped into the ceiling and corroded the plates holding the tiles. They were removed in the 1980s and kept in storage for decades. Once restoration funds were finally available, the tiles were painstakingly repaired by hand and reinstalled in 2007. The arcade is located midway within the park, which runs from Fifty-ninth through 110th streets in the center of Manhattan. The balustrade atop the arcade supports the Seventy-second Street Transverse Road.*

Left: *This three-story-high vaulted portal is the Broadway entrance to the courtyard of the Apthorp, a palatial apartment house built in 1908. It is one of three grand courtyard apartment houses built by William Waldorf Astor on Manhattan's West Side. Considered the best of the three, it is a Renaissance Revival landmark modeled on the Pitti Palace in Florence and filled with luxuriously large and richly appointed apartments. Astor, the great-grandson of a German immigrant who amassed a real-estate empire in New York, used the family fortune to build a string of famous buildings, including the Waldorf, later merged with its neighbor to become the first Waldorf-Astoria Hotel. Astor built the Apthorp for the comfortable middle class, years after he had given up his American citizenship to live the life of a gentleman in England. The Apthorp's beautiful entrance belies a nasty battle that has been going on for years between long-term tenants paying below-market rents and the current landlord, who has been trying to convert the building's residences to multimillion-dollar condominiums.*

Right: *There is more than a touch of Paris in this Upper West Side scene on Broadway. The new subway kiosk on West Seventy-second Street is a modern tribute to the Paris Metro, and the terraced and towered building on the left is the Ansonia (1904), a Gilded Age dowager still basking in her Beaux Arts glory. The original subway entrance, a block to the south of this station, opened in 1904, the year the first line of the city's subterranean system made its way uptown from City Hall to Broadway and 145th Street. The Ansonia anticipated its opening, but soon after the subway started running, it was apparent that many stations were too small to handle the ever-increasing number of passengers. The problem became extreme on this station's narrow platforms as new neighborhood developments swelled the population. The new entrance, along with additional stairways and a wider platform, was completed in 2002 and finally provided some breathing room. The Ansonia, built as a residential hotel and now filled with expensive condos, was once home to such musical legends as Toscanini, Stravinsky, and Caruso, who were able to practice undisturbed within their thick-walled suites.*

Right: Arriving at the dawn of the new millennium, the Rose Center for Earth and Space broke out of its plain brick box with a design that crossed new frontiers in time, space, and technology. This six-story glass cube holds a ninety-foot sphere that replaced the redbrick Hayden Planetarium in 2000. The old planetarium was a 1935 addition to the American Museum of Natural History (1869). Located on Manhattan's Upper West Side, it was a dark, cozy haunt for New Yorkers like Holden Caulfield, the protagonist of The Catcher in the Rye, who liked it because it never seemed to change. Flooded with light by day and emanating a blue glow by night, the Rose Center is all about a changing universe. Its architect, James Polshek, calls it a "cosmic cathedral" that inspires visitors with the wonders of the universe. The cube is made up of 736 perfectly transparent panes of glass held in place by nearly invisible stainless-steel rods. Among the attractions inside the sphere is the Sky Theater, with the world's largest virtual-reality simulator of the galaxy.

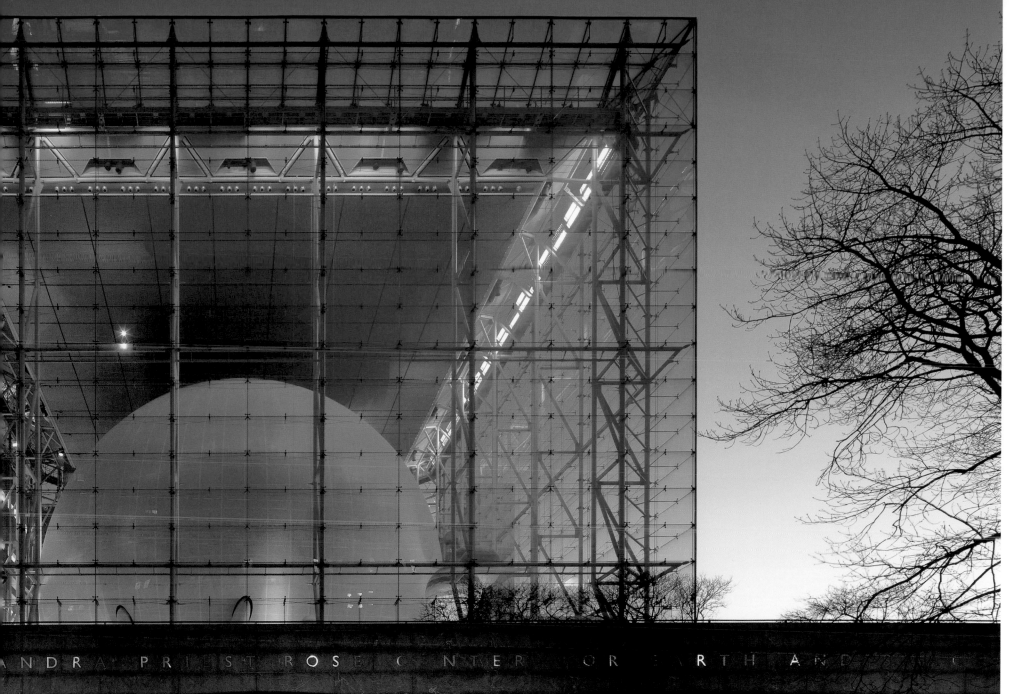

Left and above: *The Guggenheim Museum (1959) is Frank Lloyd Wright's only major work in New York City, but it is among his best-known buildings. Wright was inspired by the ancient Babylonian ziggurat, a form of pyramid, and literally turned it on its head. His design, first proposed in 1943, also turned the art world upside down. The interior of the larger structure is a single large room where paintings are hung on sloping walls along a spiraling ramp. Wright believed that the continuous circular path, which begins at the top, was a great improvement over the multiroom setup of traditional museums. But artists and art critics felt that the unusual surroundings would overwhelm the art. The museum was meant to showcase abstract art, yet even many cutting-edge artists of the day, including Willem de Kooning and Robert Motherwell, found it too radical. Today, the controversial building is recognized as its own work of art. It has been compared to a spinning top, and the museum's spiral form appears almost as animated at night. Before the Guggenheim was built, New Yorkers had never seen anything remotely like it, and certainly not on elegant Upper Fifth Avenue, where unadorned concrete exteriors had never shown their bare faces. This was—and still is—a residential neighborhood of largely traditional buildings clad in marble, granite, limestone, and, at a minimum, brick. Standing shoulder to shoulder, buildings like the ones on either side of the museum seemed to disapprove of this freestanding newcomer. At first, the famously freethinking Wright preferred an undeveloped section of the Bronx so that he could spread the museum out like he did with his Prairie-style houses. But his patron, the copper mining magnate Solomon Guggenheim, had his heart set on Manhattan. Wright settled for this site opposite Central Park to allow some breathing room for his unique design.*

Right: *Columbia University, the oldest and best-known educational institution in New York City, began as King's College in 1754 with eight students meeting in the vestry room of the original Trinity Church, built in 1698. The main campus, seen here, has been at this location on Morningside Heights in Upper Manhattan since 1897. Covering six city blocks, it includes classical buildings designed by McKim, Mead, and White, the most famous of which is the Low Memorial Library, the domed building on the right. Several of the nation's Founding Fathers and presidents, as well as many Nobel laureates and other notable figures, have been students or teachers at Columbia. But while its national and international reputation continued to grow in the twentieth century, its relations with the surrounding community of Harlem became strained as it continued to expand into the neighborhood. In 1968 student demonstrators took over five university buildings and occupied them for several days, ending their strike only after violent confrontations with the police. Tensions eased in later years as the university reached out to community leaders. In addition to the sixty-three buildings on this campus, Columbia has extensive facilities throughout the metropolitan area as well as in Europe and Asia.*

Left: *The fabled Apollo Theater on Harlem's 125th Street opened as a whites-only burlesque venue in 1914, but ever since it first invited African Americans to come onstage in 1934, it began to hold regular amateur nights, launching the careers of a star-studded roster of performers. That was the year that Ella Fitzgerald appeared here as a nervous fifteen-year-old. She had planned to dance, but at the last moment she decided to sing instead. Over the years, numerous other singers also got their start here, including Billie Holiday, Sarah Vaughan, James Brown, Ben E. King, Jackie Wilson, Michael Jackson and the Jackson Five, Jimi Hendrix, and Stevie Wonder. The Apollo still holds its amateur nights every Wednesday, and in 2010 offered a prize of $10,000 to the winner of the finals competition.*

Right: *This monumental viaduct on the edge of West Harlem was built in 1901 to carry Riverside Drive across a deep valley that runs from 125th to 135th streets. The roadway is seventy feet above the ground, and this underneath view captures the mesmerizing repetition of arched spans that has long fascinated photographers and painters. Once dark and industrial, the area under the viaduct is becoming a trendy destination. An upscale supermarket moved in nearby a few years ago, and new restaurants have also arrived. Dramatic changes will occur when Columbia University, whose main campus is a few blocks to the south, begins building an additional campus on seventeen acres adjacent to the viaduct. Listed on the National Register of Historic Places, the viaduct will become a major design feature of the new campus.*

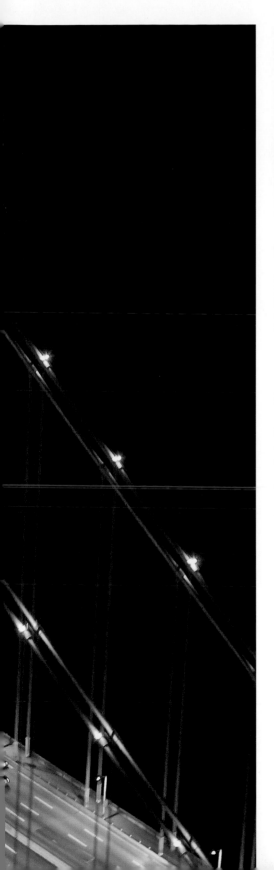

Left: The modernist architect Le Corbusier proclaimed the George Washington "the most beautiful bridge in the world," largely because of the bare steel frame of its towers. This signature feature was the result of economic necessity, rather than part of the original design. The engineer, Othmar Ammann, and architect, Cass Gilbert, intended the towers to be sheathed in granite. But as the bridge neared completion in 1931, the Great Depression squeezed the construction budget and they decided to leave the steelwork exposed without any cladding or architectural flourishes.

Above: The deck of the George Washington Bridge rises 212 feet above the shimmering Hudson River. It is the only Hudson River crossing between New York City (right) and New Jersey (left). The 3,500-foot-long main span was the longest in the world when it was built. One of seventy-six bridges crossing New York City waters, it has a commanding presence that can be seen for miles.

Above: *From its debut in 1904, the New York City subway system has grown to become one of the largest public transportation systems in the world. With 842 miles of track and 466 stations operating twenty-four hours a day, it carries more passengers than the combination of all other mass-transit rail systems in the United States. An average of five million riders use the system each weekday, with a larger number on weekends. All that traffic requires lots of space to store and repair trains, and this huge yard, located on 207th Street at the northern tip of Manhattan along the Harlem River, is just one of nearly two dozen yards throughout the city. It also provides room for buses.*

Right: *A moment in baseball history is captured here as the new Yankee Stadium (left) shines while its historic predecessor (right) is in partial demolition. Opened in 2009, the new ballpark cost $1.3 billion. Controversy arose over the substantial amount of public funds contributed to the project, but Yankee fans prevailed, including former mayor Rudy Giuliani, who made the deal. The old stadium was built in 1923, the year the Yankees acquired a young Babe Ruth. The Yankees previously shared a stadium in Manhattan, but Ruth and his teammates drew huge crowds to the Bronx. Some longtime Yankee fans are preserving memories of the old stadium by purchasing salvaged seats and even freeze-dried sod taken from the old field. The soccer field on the right is one of the public recreation areas the Yankees were required to build after the new stadium gobbled up a public park.*

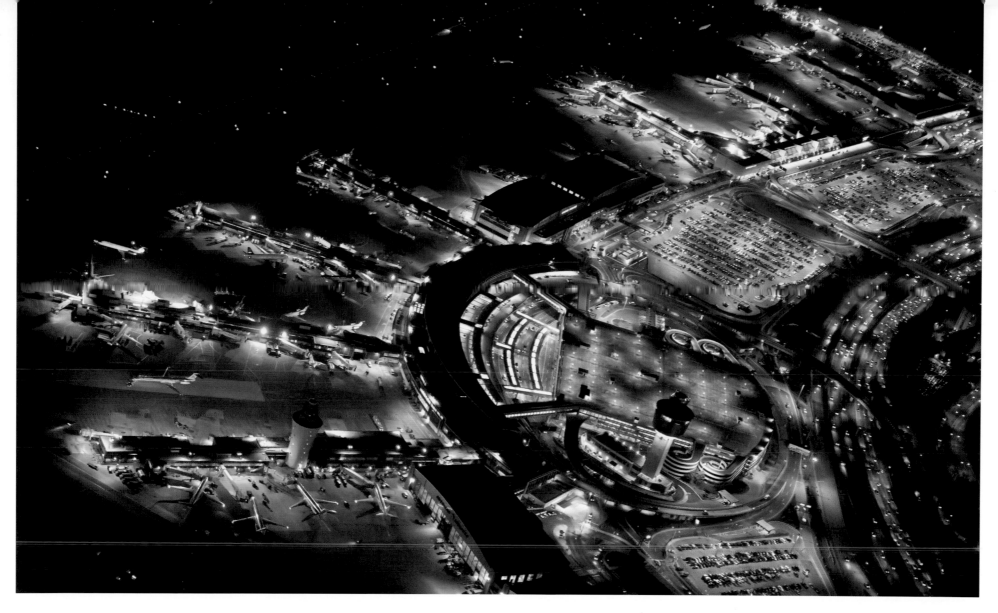

Left: A giant alien bug climbs up these circular towers to board a waiting spaceship in the 1997 film Men in Black. The towers have a more serious place in history as part of the New York State Pavilion, the architectural star of the 1964–65 World's Fair in Flushing Meadows. Designed by renowned architect Philip Johnson, the building includes a large elliptical base, the "Tent of Tomorrow," originally covered with multicolored, translucent plastic panels that made up the world's largest suspension roof. The towers held observation platforms reached by glass-walled elevators. On the right is the Unisphere, another landmark from the fair. Flushing Meadows, named for the nearby Flushing River, was a large tidal expanse, used for decades as a refuse dump and cleaned up for the 1939–40 World's Fair. Although neither fair was financially successful, the 1964–65 fair was hugely popular, drawing more than fifty million visitors over its two-year duration. The land was dedicated as a park in 1967, and remains the largest one in Queens. It also includes Citi Field, the New York Mets' new baseball stadium, and the U.S. Tennis Center, home of the U.S. Open.

Above: Many of the names given to public places are honorary tributes, but LaGuardia Airport was named after the man who actually created it. In the 1930s, the colorful and forceful New York City mayor Fiorello LaGuardia was outraged that travelers flying to New York had to land in Newark, New Jersey, because the airlines did not use New York's only municipal airport, Floyd Bennett Field in Brooklyn. On a famous flight of his own, the mayor, pointing to his ticket to New York, convinced the pilot to land at the Brooklyn field and later got some of the airlines to offer flights there. These flights proved unviable because it took too long for passengers to travel between Manhattan and this site deep in Brooklyn. Undeterred, the mayor secured $45 million in federal funds to build LaGuardia Airport on a waterfront site in Queens, which was closer to Manhattan. More than 350 acres were added with landfill, including runways projecting into Flushing Bay; it opened in 1939. While John F. Kennedy Airport, built in 1948, would grow much larger, LaGuardia is still one of the busiest airports in the country, handling twenty-three million passengers a year.

135

Left: *Although it is not the most famous bridge in New York, the Queensboro Bridge, also known as the Fifty-ninth Street Bridge, has its own song. Simon and Garfunkel, both from Queens, gave it that honor with their 1966 hit "Fifty-ninth Street Bridge Song (Feelin' Groovy)." The bridge has a lot more going for it as well. Engineers consider it one of the greatest cantilever bridges in the history of American bridge design. It opened in 1909 as the third span over the East River, long after the Brooklyn Bridge in 1883, six years after the Williamsburg Bridge, and just nine months before the Manhattan Bridge. The Queensboro's massive, double-decked trusses cross the river between Fifty-ninth Street in Manhattan and Long Island City in Queens. This view looks toward Queens, a mostly low-rise borough that nonetheless has New York's tallest skyscraper outside of Manhattan, the fifty-story One Court Square (1989), seen here between the bridge towers. On the far right is the Manhattan tower of the Roosevelt Island Tram. Its brightly lit, boxy terminal can be seen on the island to the left of the bridge towers.*

Right: *Roosevelt Island, formerly known as Welfare Island, is a sliver of land between Manhattan (right) and Queens (left) that was a place of last resort for the poor and sick in the nineteenth century. Shades of the past still exist in the fascinating ruins of two historic hospitals. One of them, a Gothic castle built in 1856 for smallpox victims, is illuminated at the dark tip of the island. Designed by James Renwick, architect of St. Patrick's Cathedral, it is preserved as the Renwick Ruin. Most of the two-mile-long island is now a much happier place. Beginning in the 1970s, it was transformed into a new urban community where some 12,000 reside.*

Some of the newer residents live in the Octagon, an apartment house built in 2006 next to the preserved octagon tower of the former New York Lunatic Asylum (1834). While the Queensboro Bridge passes over the island, it no longer provides direct access. An elevator from the center of the bridge to the island carried people up and down until the 1950s, when a smaller bridge was built directly to the island from Queens. An aerial tramway strung a connection to midtown Manhattan in 1976 and the Roosevelt Island subway station opened in 1989. More than 100 feet underground, it is the deepest station in the system.

Left: *The Narrows, the shortest distance across New York Bay between Staten Island (left) and Brooklyn (right), was only a relative term for the builders of the Verrazano-Narrows Bridge. To span it, engineers had to design the longest suspension bridge in the world with 693-foot-high towers that could accommodate the curvature of the earth. They also faced intense opposition from the Brooklyn side, where more than 8,000 residents would be displaced by construction of the highway links to the bridge. Planned for nearly fifteen years, construction finally began in 1959 and was not completed until 1964. Although longer spans have been built in Europe and Asia, the Verrazano, with a center span of 4,260 feet, is still the longest suspension bridge in the United States. Lit at night, its slim profile is a glittering landmark that can be admired from throughout the city, including from Manhattan, seen here in the background. Some 50,000 runners cross this bridge from Staten Island each November at the start of the New York City Marathon.*

Right: *Every American schoolchild learns that the Statue of Liberty was a gift from the French in celebration of the centennial of the 1776 Declaration of Independence. The tablet she holds is inscribed with that date. Not as well known is the fact that French republicans had their own agenda. Chafing under the reign of Napoléon III, they came up with the idea for the gift in 1865 as a way to focus attention on freedom from the monarchy. The French completed the statue in time for the United States' 1876 centennial, but it took another decade before Americans raised the funds to build the pedestal and erect both statue and pedestal in the harbor in 1886. A few years later, as millions of immigrants began to arrive at the new immigration center that opened on Ellis Island in 1892, the statue became a stirring symbol of welcome. In 1903, a plaque was installed inside the pedestal, bearing the now-famous lines by Emma Lazarus: "Give me your tired, your poor, your huddled masses yearning to breathe free . . ." This panoramic view spans from the Chrysler Building (far right) to Ellis Island (far left).*

ACKNOWLEDGMENTS

Evan Joseph

This book is dedicated to my father, for the love and patience to raise an artist; to my mother, who is always on my side; to my brother, my biggest fan; to my beautiful wife, my muse and my partner; and to my children, my greatest joy, with apologies for all the late nights shooting when I missed bath time and story time.

I gratefully acknowledge the support of all my wonderful clients who allowed me to scale the rooftop labyrinths of their buildings and held my belt as I dangled off the edges to capture their truly unique views.

Marcia Reiss

To my husband, Charlie, for his expert New York City insight and unwavering support. Many thanks also to Evan Joseph for his fantastic photos and to David Salmo for a wonderful design and editing job. It was a pleasure working together on this great project.

PICTURE CREDITS

All photos by Evan Joseph Uhlfelder, with the exception of the following pages: 8, 9, 12, 13, 14, 15 (Bettmann/Corbis); 10 (Museum of the City of New York/Corbis); 11 (Library of Congress, LC-DIG-pga-03106).

Right: *The Canyon of Heroes, lined with tall buildings along Lower Broadway, has been a parade route for heroes of many different endeavors, from wars to space travel and sports. Office workers shower the parade with tons of confetti and shredded paper tossed out the building windows. Plaques embedded in the sidewalks are engraved with the names of the honorees throughout the years. The tower in the background is the tallest in the Wall Street area (see page 36).*